The Macmillan

Atlas of the Future

The Macmillan

Atlas of the Future

edited by Ian Pearson

Macmillan • USA

Published by Macmillan Books
Macmillan General Reference USA
Macmillan Publishing USA
1633 Broadway
New York
NY 10019-6785
USA

First published 1998

10 9 8 7 6 5 4 3 2 1

Published in the UK by Routledge

Produced by
Myriad Editions Limited
52 Maple Street
London WIP 5GE
myriad@dircon.co.uk

Edited and coordinated for Myriad Editions by
Anne Benewick and Candida Lacey
Graphic design by Corinne Pearlman
Text design by Pentagram Design Limited
Maps created by All Terrain Mapping,
West Molesey, Surrey, UK

Printed in Hong Kong by Phoenix Offset

Library of Congress Cataloging-in-Publication Data

The Macmillan atlas of the future / edited by Ian Pearson.

p. cm.

Includes technology calendar , world table and index.

Contents: pt. 1. The future of the earth -- pt. 2. The future of people --
pt. 3. The future of resources -- pt. 4. The future of communications -- pt.
5. The future of globalization -- pt. 6. Into the unknown.

ISBN 0-02-862088-7 (hardcover) . -- ISBN 0-02-862089-5 (pbk.)

1. Atlases. 2. Forecasting--Maps.

G1021 .M15 1998 <G&M>

912--DC21   98-18102
                                             CIP
                                             MAPS

Contents

Introduction

The past is gone – it is history, a topic for study and discussion, just memories. We can't change it, though we may be able to conceal events or change perceptions. The past defines our starting point as we move toward tomorrow and it is a source of useful planning information to help us on our way.

The present is simply the realization of decisions made in the past. We can enjoy it and experience it but again we can't change it. Every action that occurs now is the result of an earlier action, however recently it occurred. It is an experiential boundary, a mixture of past experience and future planning.

But the future is where we will spend the rest of our lives, and we can control it – to some extent. It is the only part of our lives we can affect. We need to know the options open to us, and how to determine what happens. If you believe in fate, that the future is fixed, then there is nothing you can do about it. You might as well just sit back and watch it happen. But the future is not fixed. Some of it is undoubtedly outside our control, other bits are entirely up to us, most is somewhere in between.

People have always tried to discern what is likely to happen in order to plan for it. Whether it is reading tea leaves or running computer simulations, the purpose is basically the same. Techniques differ and some are no more than superstition, but even with the best methods, precision is impossible for most things. There is always some factor that is a matter of chance or depends on choice, but it is still usually worthwhile to outline the range of possibilities. A steering wheel is of little use without a view of the road ahead. If we don't like what we see straight ahead, we can take evasive action. If we have also studied the side roads, then we can do even better and aim for the things we like best or dislike least. Without this second part of the planning, we may end up with an even worse future than the one we had tried to avoid.

So what might happen tomorrow? How will we live in the years to come? What environment should we be planning for? What is everyone else planning to do and what will the world look like as a result? What are the threats? Where are the opportunities? Importantly, what is outside our control and what can we change? These are the questions that made us write this book. We have tried to show where things will go, taking into account current trends and decisions already made. We are showing you what lies straight ahead and down some of the side roads. But the route that the future will actually take is partly up to you.

Ian Pearson
April 1998

The Future of the
Earth

in 1 million, billion, billion years
FUTURE OF AN OPEN, FLAT, OR LONG-LIVED, CLOSED UNIVERSE
years since the Big Bang
logarithmic scale

The closer astronomers come to observing the beginning of time, the more accurately they can predict the future of the universe.

Space telescopes, like the Hubble, capture light left by galaxies billions of years ago. In 2007, the Next Generation Space Telescope may see the first galaxies forming, and glimpse the first and last days of the universe (see **Space Exploration**, pages 88–9).

Today, the observable radius of the universe is about 15 billion light years. Most astronomers agree that the universe started with a Big Bang between 10 and 20 billion years ago. Most expect its evolution to be stable for at least 100 billion years. There are three theories for what might happen after that. An "open" universe would expand forever to an infinite size. A "flat" universe would expand ever more slowly, eventually reaching a finite size. A "closed" universe would collapse back to a point similar to the original Big Bang, when a new Big Bang might occur and a new universe emerge.

Sources: see pages 122–5

the present

100 billion years into the future: The Milky Way will run out of starmaking material and cease to produce new stars.

100,000 billion years into the future: All other galaxies will cease to produce new stars. When the last generation of stars runs out of fuel, the universe will begin to grow dark.

Galaxies will shed stars as they interact during orbits around a central black hole. This process of galactic evaporation will occur over a period of 100,000 billion years.

logarithmic scale

10^{10} 10^{12} 10^{14} 10^{16} 10^{18} 10^{2}

1 billion, billion years into the future: Most stars will have been ejected from galaxies. Any remaining will have been absorbed by the central massive black hole.

15 billion years ago: Our universe formed in a Big Bang. All forces including gravity were united into one Superforce. At 10^{-50} years after the Big Bang, the Superforce separated into gravity and a Grand United Force. At this stage, modern physics can be applied to the understanding of the evolution of the universe.

10^{-7}
One second after the Big Bang.

10^{20}

10^{10}

10^{0}

10^{-10}

10^{-20}

10^{-30}

10^{-40}

10^{-50}

Inflationary period: The universe rapidly expanded in size by 10^{50} or 100 trillion, trillion, trillion, trillion times.

10,000 years after the Big Bang: the first atoms were formed.

1.5×10^{10}
the present

10^{11}
100 billion years into the future.

10^{12}
1,000 billion or one trillion years into the future.

years since the Big Bang

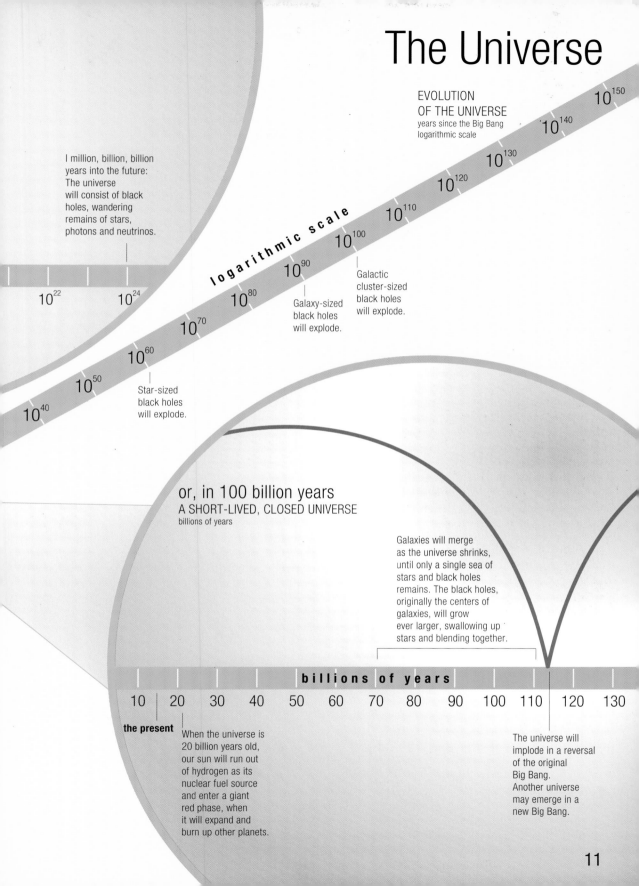

The Universe

EVOLUTION
OF THE UNIVERSE
years since the Big Bang
logarithmic scale

10^{150}

10^{140}

10^{130}

10^{120}

10^{110}

logarithmic scale

10^{100}

10^{90}

10^{80}

10^{70}

10^{60}

10^{50}

10^{40}

10^{22}

10^{24}

I million, billion, billion years into the future: The universe will consist of black holes, wandering remains of stars, photons and neutrinos.

Galactic cluster-sized black holes will explode.

Galaxy-sized black holes will explode.

Star-sized black holes will explode.

or, in 100 billion years
A SHORT-LIVED, CLOSED UNIVERSE
billions of years

Galaxies will merge as the universe shrinks, until only a single sea of stars and black holes remains. The black holes, originally the centers of galaxies, will grow ever larger, swallowing up stars and blending together.

billions of years

10   20   30   40   50   60   70   80   90   100   110   120   130

the present

When the universe is 20 billion years old, our sun will run out of hydrogen as its nuclear fuel source and enter a giant red phase, when it will expand and burn up other planets.

The universe will implode in a reversal of the original Big Bang. Another universe may emerge in a new Big Bang.

In 2000, NASA plans to launch missile attacks against two asteroids on earth-crossing orbits. These missions will mark the first step by humans toward defending the earth from a threat now widely blamed for the extinction of the dinosaurs.

A small asteroid may collide with the earth every ten years or so, and cause little or no damage. A 10km asteroid or comet would obliterate most living species. A giant comet, the 50km Hale-Bopp, lit up our skies in 1997. Between 1998 and 2020, at least a hundred comets and asteroids will pass less than 10 million miles from the earth. There may be many more that have yet to be identified.

Schemes to protect the earth against catastrophic collisions include high-powered early warning systems of telescopes and radars. Nuclear missiles may be used to shatter an advancing asteroid, but this might only break it up into smaller, still lethal fragments. Alternatively, controlled explosions may be used, or thrusters may be attached to an asteroid to deflect it from its collision course.

Comets and asteroids are the debris from the formation of the solar system. Our own debris, discarded in previous space missions, threatens space exploration. Thousands of objects are orbiting the earth at 15km per second – a speed that transforms discarded bolts into lethal objects. Larger pieces of "space junk" may be exploded or deflected out of the earth's orbit. Ultimately, all spacecraft may be designed to crash back to the earth or burn up on re-entry into the atmosphere.

Sources: see pages 122–5

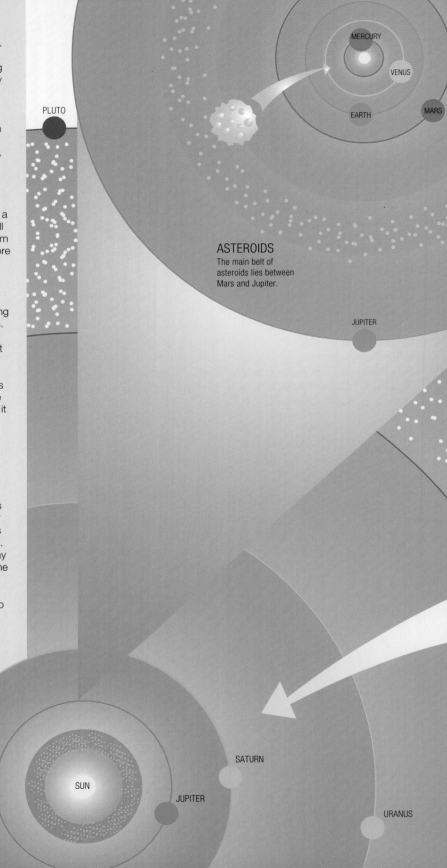

PLUTO

MERCURY

VENUS

EARTH

MARS

ASTEROIDS
The main belt of asteroids lies between Mars and Jupiter.

JUPITER

SUN

JUPITER

SATURN

URANUS

Spaceguard

2000 PROTECTING THE EARTH

Two asteroids, 1986JK (1km) and Toutatis (3km), will be intercepted. This will be a first step towards the ultimate aim of deflecting asteroids or comets from crossing earth's orbit.

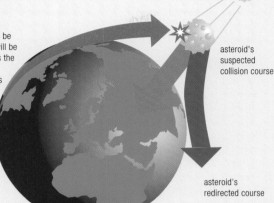

asteroid's suspected collision course

asteroid's redirected course

OORT CLOUD

Over the millennia, some comets have moved out to form the Oort Cloud, which extends as far as 0.5 to 1 light years.

KUIPER BELT

Comets lie in the Kuiper Belt, beyond the orbit of Neptune.

NEPTUNE

RISK FACTORS

Frequency of asteroids or comets entering earth's orbit, by size (diameter), and potential damage in any collision

● *every 10 years*
0.01km: little or no damage

● *every 100 years*
0.06km: considerable damage

● *every 1,000 years*
0.1km: widespread destruction up to 20km from center of explosion

● *every 5,000 years*
0.5km: damage equivalent to 100-200 megaton nuclear weapon

● *every 300,000 years*
1km: destruction up to hundreds of km from center of explosion

● *every 2 million years*
2km: massive destruction and possible nuclear winter

● *every 10 million years*
5km: global catastrophe and mass extinctions

● *every 100 million year*s
10km: obliteration of most living species – a similar-sized body caused extinction of dinosaurs

● *1 billion years*
50km: size of Hale-Bopp, seen in 1997

Earthquakes signal rock movement. The irregular shapes they create across the globe mark the surface boundaries of the earth's tectonic plates. When plates move apart they grow in area and new ocean floor, such as the Atlantic Ocean, is created.

When plates collide they create wider earthquake zones like those around the Pacific Ocean and the north east area of the Indian Ocean, and form explosive volcanoes. During plate collision on the floor of the ocean, the old floor is subducted – literally led under – back into the interior of the earth. Continents are not dense enough to be subducted: continental collisions are marked by high mountain ranges, such as the Himalayas, where India has rammed into Asia. Sometimes, plates simply slide past one another, as along the San Andreas Fault in California.

Laser measurements of present-day plate motions show that the Atlantic Ocean is getting wider and the Pacific Ocean and Mediterranean are shrinking. They also show that a new plate, the Somali plate, is gradually breaking away from East Africa.

Present-day movement can be extrapolated many years into the future. In 100 million years, Australia may have collided with Asia. The Somali plate may have detached from Africa, the Atlantic may be wider and the Mediterranean may have vanished.

Looking 200 million years ahead, some geologists predict that the Somali plate will collide with India, bringing Antarctica close to Australia and the Americas closer to both. The continents may form one huge supercontinent, a process which has happened probably three times in the past 750 million years, the most recent being 250 million years ago.

Sources: see pages 122–5

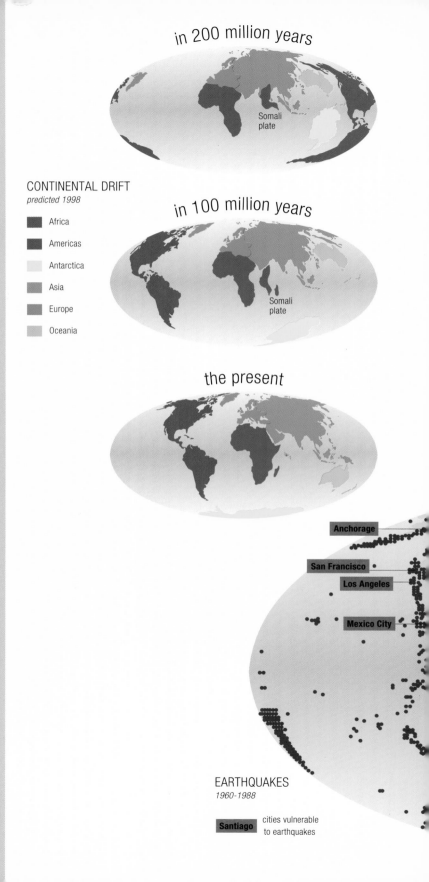

in 200 million years

Somali plate

CONTINENTAL DRIFT
predicted 1998

- Africa
- Americas
- Antarctica
- Asia
- Europe
- Oceania

in 100 million years

Somali plate

the present

Anchorage

San Francisco

Los Angeles

Mexico City

EARTHQUAKES
1960-1988

Santiago — cities vulnerable to earthquakes

Faultlines

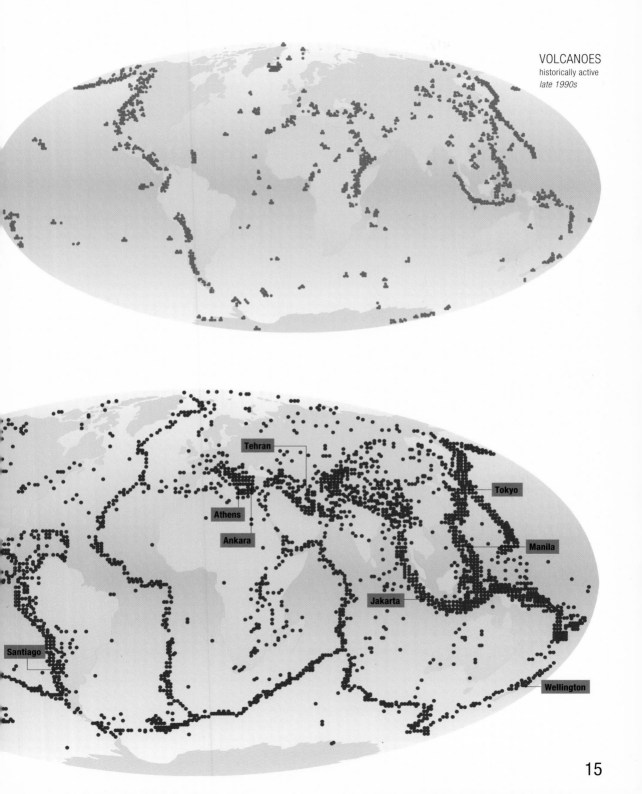

VOLCANOES
historically active
late 1990s

Tehran

Tokyo

Athens

Ankara

Manila

Jakarta

Santiago

Wellington

Without human intervention, the natural glacial cycle will eventually lead to another ice age, culminating in about 100,000 AD. In this scenario, which assumes global warming becomes a distant memory, the sea level would sink by 100 to 120 meters. The earth would return to the peak glaciation of 18,000 years ago.

In the late 1990s, as the climate warms (see **Global Warming**, pages 18–19), the global sea level is rising two millimeters a year, on average, or two centimeters each decade. Sea water expands when the ocean temperature rises and ice sheets melt. Over millions of years tectonic forces change the volume of sea water in ocean basins, which also influences the global sea level (see **Faultlines**, pages 14–15).

By 2100, global sea levels could rise by anything between 15 and 95 centimeters. The effects of such an increase, projected by the Intergovernmental Panel on Climate Change (IPCC), could flood low-lying areas such as coastal Bangladesh or the Florida Everglades. Rising sea temperatures may also increase the number of coastal storms.

The thick ice sheets on Greenland and Antarctica will take a long time to melt, though some scientists argue that the west Antarctic ice sheet is already unstable. If it were to vanish, global sea levels would rise by six meters. It would take severe global warming – over a few thousand years – to melt all the earth's thick ice completely. This would raise sea levels by 60 to 70 meters, inundating large coastal areas.

Sources:
see pages 122–5

GLOBAL WARMING
Flooding caused by
4.5 meter rise in sea level
Florida, USA

flooded area

USA

Florida

Orlando

Tampa

Miami

ASIA

AUSTRALIA

ANTARCTICA

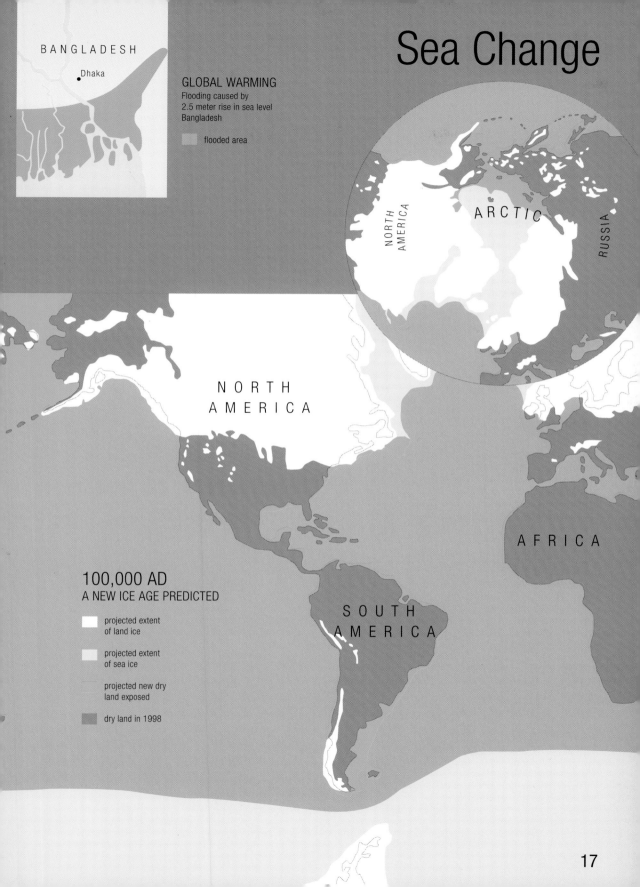

Sea Change

BANGLADESH

Dhaka

GLOBAL WARMING
Flooding caused by
2.5 meter rise in sea level
Bangladesh

flooded area

ARCTIC

NORTH
AMERICA

RUSSIA

NORTH
AMERICA

AFRICA

100,000 AD
A NEW ICE AGE PREDICTED

projected extent
of land ice

projected extent
of sea ice

projected new dry
land exposed

dry land in 1998

SOUTH
AMERICA

The world's climate is getting warmer. Industrial activity is increasing the concentration of greenhouse gases in the atmosphere. This is probably the main cause of global warming.

Carbon dioxide makes up over half of all greenhouse gases; others include nitrous oxide, chlorofluorocarbons (CFCs), methane, and water vapor.

In 1992, most countries signed the Framework Convention on Climate Change at the Earth Summit in Rio de Janeiro. Its goal, to reduce emissions of greenhouse gases to a level that would not interfere with the earth's climate, now looks difficult to achieve. Most signatories are not living up to their commitment; the USA refused to sign. Projections of global energy use in 2010 predict that 35 percent more fossil fuels will be burned than in 1996 (see **Energy**, pages 52–3); the Intergovernmental Panel on Climate Change (IPCC) believes that, simply to stabilize greenhouse gases at 1992 levels, carbon dioxide emissions need to be cut by 60 percent.

This map, from a NASA model of the IPCC 1995 forecast, predicts climate change in 2100 if carbon dioxide emissions continue to increase. Most warming will be at higher latitudes with smaller changes near the equator. Winters are likely to warm more than summers.

Sources: see pages 122–5

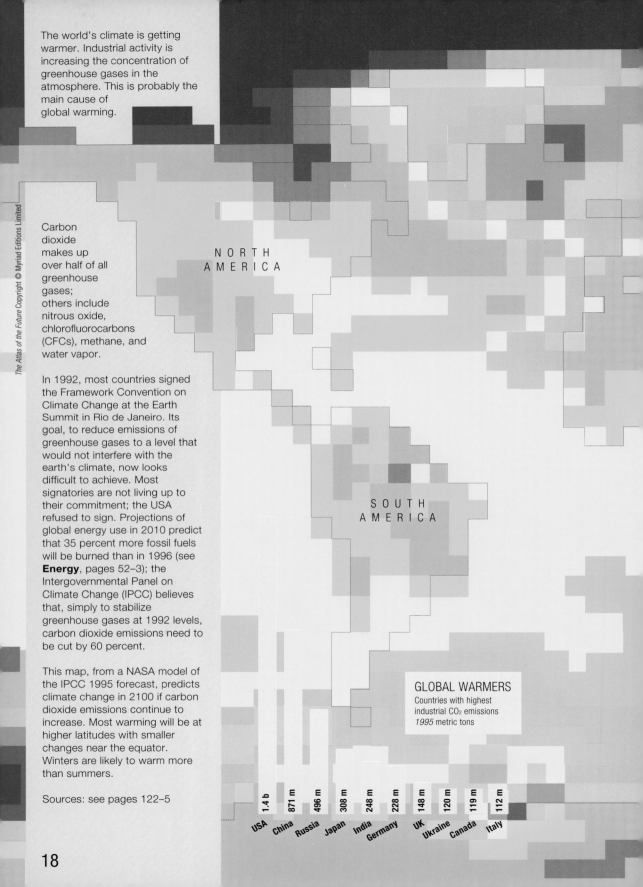

NORTH AMERICA

SOUTH AMERICA

GLOBAL WARMERS
Countries with highest industrial CO$_2$ emissions
1995 metric tons

USA	China	Russia	Japan	India	Germany	UK	Ukraine	Canada	Italy
1.4 b	871 m	496 m	308 m	248 m	228 m	148 m	120 m	119 m	112 m

Global Warming

E U R O P E

A S I A

A F R I C A

2010

China's CO_2 emissions will double
between 1992 and 2010 as its
population grows and economy expands

AUSTRALIA

2100
GLOBAL WARMING
Projected temperature changes
if concentration of carbon dioxide
in the atmosphere doubles compared
with 1996 levels
projected 1996 degrees centigrade

- more than 6°C increase
- 5°C – 6°C increase
- 4°C – 5°C increase
- 3°C – 4°C increase
- 2°C – 3°C increase
- 1°C – 2°C increase
- little or no change
- 0°C – 1°C decrease
- 1°C – 2°C decrease
- 2°C – 3°C decrease
- 3°C – 4°C decrease
- more than 4°C decrease

A N T A R C T I C A

At ground level, ozone is a major pollutant. High up in the stratosphere, however, a thin layer of ozone protects us from solar ultraviolet radiation. Its depletion increases the risk of skin cancer and depresses our immune systems.

During the late 1970s, a hole in the ozone layer was discovered over Antarctica. Up to 60 percent of the ozone is destroyed every September, leaving a hole that persists for many weeks. A similar but smaller effect occurs in the Arctic.

Chlorine and bromide atoms, found in synthetic compounds such as chlorofluorocarbons (CFCs) and halons, accelerate ozone loss. CFCs are a common industrial product, used in air conditioners, refrigeration systems, aerosols, foams, and solvents. Some can remain in the atmosphere for up to 200 years.

In 1987, the United Nations' Montreal Protocol called for reductions in CFC releases; a series of amendments in 1992 called for faster reductions. Between 1984 and 1992 the use of CFCs and halons decreased by 90 percent in countries of the Organization for Economic Co-operation and Development (OECD). If the reductions continue worldwide, atmospheric ozone should return to natural levels by 2050, and the Antarctic ozone hole will be healed.

Sources: see pages 122–5

The Atlas of the Future Copyright © Myriad Editions Limited

OZONE EATERS
Number of years in the atmosphere and ozone depletion potential (ODP) *1998*

The ozone depletion potential (ODP) ranking combines the lifetime of ions in the atmosphere with their relative strength in destroying ozone.

Although methyl bromide is 40 to 50 times more destructive to ozone than CFC-11, it lasts no longer than two years in the atmosphere, so their effects – and ODP rankings – are comparable.

Hydrofluorocarbons (HCFCs) have a relatively low ODP. They were introduced to replace CFCs.

200 years
CFC-114 (**ODP 1.0**)

120 years
CFC-12 (**ODP 1.0**)

80-100 years
CFC-113 (**ODP 0.8**)
halon 1301 (**ODP 10.0**)

60 years
CFC-11 (**ODP 1.0**)

25 years
halon 1211 (**ODP 3.0**)
halon 2402 (**ODP 6.0**)

15-20 years
HCFC-22 (**ODP 0.05**)

1-2 years
methyl bromide (**ODP 0.7**

2010

SOUTH AMERICA

ozone hole

1992

SOUTH AMERICA

ozone hole

Ozone

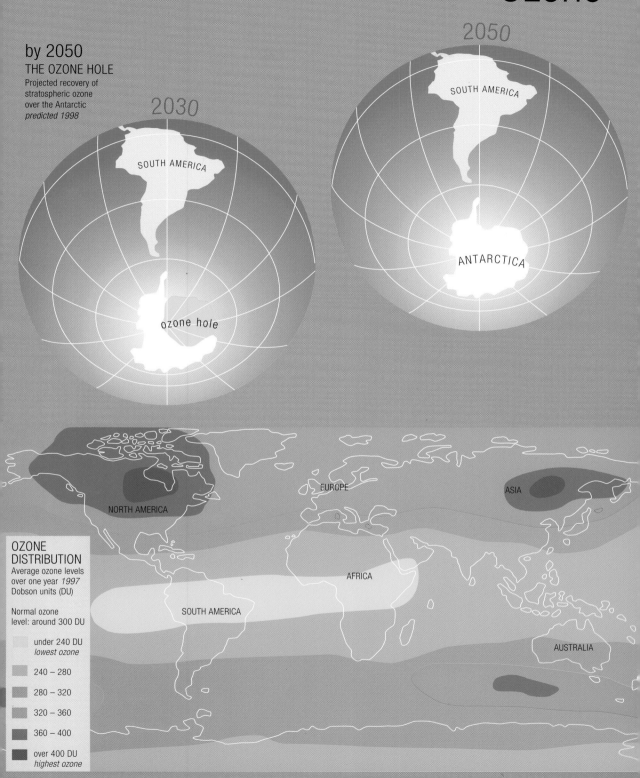

by 2050
THE OZONE HOLE
Projected recovery of
stratospheric ozone
over the Antarctic
predicted 1998

2030

2050

SOUTH AMERICA

SOUTH AMERICA

ozone hole

ANTARCTICA

EUROPE

ASIA

NORTH AMERICA

AFRICA

SOUTH AMERICA

AUSTRALIA

OZONE
DISTRIBUTION
Average ozone levels
over one year *1997*
Dobson units (DU)

Normal ozone
level: around 300 DU

- under 240 DU *lowest ozone*
- 240 – 280
- 280 – 320
- 320 – 360
- 360 – 400
- over 400 DU *highest ozone*

The Future of
People

Population growth is steadily slowing down. The United Nations projection for world population in 2050 is now 470 million lower than it was in 1994.

Worldwide, women are having fewer children. In much of the rich world, fertility rates are continuing to decline. In some European countries, death rates are outnumbering birth rates; without immigration, the population of Spain, for example, would decline.

The rate of growth may be slowing down, but the total numbers continue to rise. Each year, we add 80 million, the equivalent of the population of Germany, to the world total. In 2000, there will be more than six billion people in the world. During the 2060s, there may be 10 billion.

In the poor world, large families remain the primary means of economic security. As the map shows, Africa's rate of growth is expected to increase during the first half of the 21st century. In some developing countries, populations are likely to triple or even quadruple. By 2040, the population of India will be larger than the population of China; by 2050, nearly one-third of the world's population will live in these two countries alone.

Worldwide the population is ageing as well as growing (see **Lifetimes**, pages 26–7). Each month, the world's population of over 65-year-olds increases by more than 800,000. By 2010, this monthly increase is likely to be over a million.

Sources: see pages 122–5

1986 **5** billion
1998 **6** billion
by 2011 **7** billion
by 2025 **8** billion
by 2042 **9** billion
by 2060s **10** billion

ATLANTIC OCEAN

by 2060s
WORLD POPULATION
billion
projected 1998

In 1801, the world population was 1 billion. It took 158 years to reach 3 billion, in 1959. By 1998, in less than 40 years, this figure doubled to 6 billion.

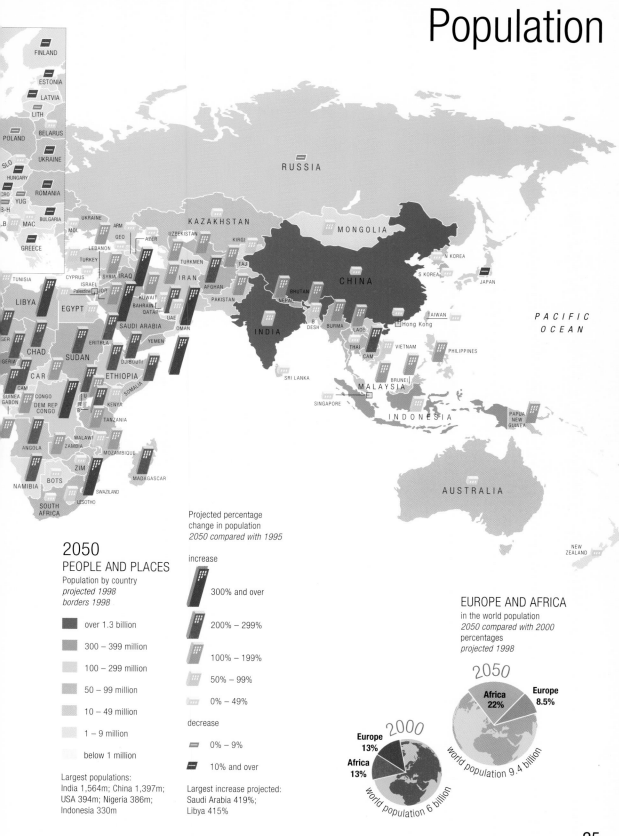

Population

RUSSIA
KAZAKHSTAN
MONGOLIA
CHINA
INDIA
JAPAN
AUSTRALIA
INDONESIA
NEW ZEALAND

PACIFIC OCEAN

2050
PEOPLE AND PLACES
Population by country
projected 1998
borders 1998

- over 1.3 billion
- 300 – 399 million
- 100 – 299 million
- 50 – 99 million
- 10 – 49 million
- 1 – 9 million
- below 1 million

Largest populations:
India 1,564m; China 1,397m;
USA 394m; Nigeria 386m;
Indonesia 330m

Projected percentage
change in population
2050 compared with 1995

increase
- 300% and over
- 200% – 299%
- 100% – 199%
- 50% – 99%
- 0% – 49%

decrease
- 0% – 9%
- 10% and over

Largest increase projected:
Saudi Arabia 419%;
Libya 415%

EUROPE AND AFRICA
in the world population
2050 compared with 2000
percentages
projected 1998

2050
Africa 22%   Europe 8.5%
world population 9.4 billion

2000
Europe 13%
Africa 13%
world population 6 billion

25

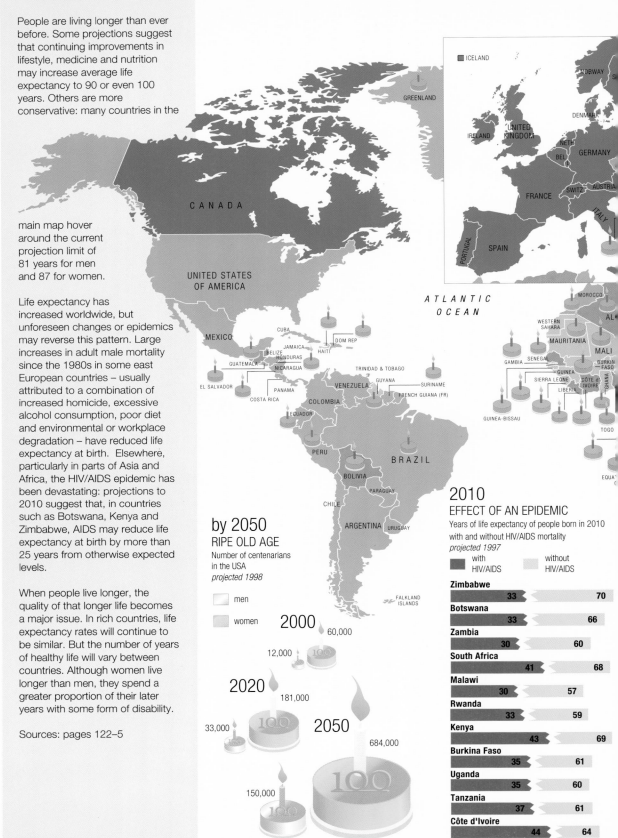

People are living longer than ever before. Some projections suggest that continuing improvements in lifestyle, medicine and nutrition may increase average life expectancy to 90 or even 100 years. Others are more conservative: many countries in the main map hover around the current projection limit of 81 years for men and 87 for women.

Life expectancy has increased worldwide, but unforeseen changes or epidemics may reverse this pattern. Large increases in adult male mortality since the 1980s in some east European countries – usually attributed to a combination of increased homicide, excessive alcohol consumption, poor diet and environmental or workplace degradation – have reduced life expectancy at birth. Elsewhere, particularly in parts of Asia and Africa, the HIV/AIDS epidemic has been devastating: projections to 2010 suggest that, in countries such as Botswana, Kenya and Zimbabwe, AIDS may reduce life expectancy at birth by more than 25 years from otherwise expected levels.

When people live longer, the quality of that longer life becomes a major issue. In rich countries, life expectancy rates will continue to be similar. But the number of years of healthy life will vary between countries. Although women live longer than men, they spend a greater proportion of their later years with some form of disability.

Sources: pages 122–5

ATLANTIC OCEAN

ICELAND

by 2050
RIPE OLD AGE
Number of centenarians in the USA
projected 1998

☐ men
▨ women

2000
60,000
12,000

2020
181,000
33,000

2050
684,000
150,000

2010
EFFECT OF AN EPIDEMIC
Years of life expectancy of people born in 2010 with and without HIV/AIDS mortality
projected 1997

▮ with HIV/AIDS ▯ without HIV/AIDS

Country	with HIV/AIDS	without HIV/AIDS
Zimbabwe	33	70
Botswana	33	66
Zambia	30	60
South Africa	41	68
Malawi	30	57
Rwanda	33	59
Kenya	43	69
Burkina Faso	35	61
Uganda	35	60
Tanzania	37	61
Côte d'Ivoire	44	64

Lifetimes

FINLAND
EST
LATVIA
LITH
POLAND
BELARUS
SLO
UKRAINE
UNGARY
C
ROMANIA
H
YUG
M
ALB
BULGARIA
GREECE

RUSSIA

TUNISIA
LEB
MOL
UKRAINE
KAZAKHSTAN
MONGOLIA
N KOREA
S KOREA
JAPAN

GEO
A
AZER
UZBEKISTAN
KIRGISTAN
TURKEY
CYPRUS
SYRIA
TURKMENISTAN
TAJ
AFGHANISTAN
CHINA

LIBYA
EGYPT
ISRAEL
Palestine
JOR
IRAQ
KUWAIT
IRAN
PAKISTAN
BHUTAN
NEPAL
TAIWAN

PACIFIC
OCEAN

SAUDI
ARABIA
QATAR
BAHRAIN
UAE
OMAN
INDIA
BANGLADESH
BURMA
LAOS
THAI
Hong Kong

NIGER
CHAD
SUDAN
ERITREA
YEMEN
DJIBOUTI
PHILIPPINES
KIRIBATI

NIGERIA
CAM
CAR
ETHIOPIA
SOMALIA
SRI LANKA
CAM
VIETNAM
BRUNEI

GABON
CONGO
U
R
B
KENYA
SINGAPORE
MALAYSIA

DEM REP
CONGO
TANZANIA
INDONESIA
PAPUA
NEW
GUINEA

ANGOLA
ZAMBIA
MALAWI
MADAGASCAR

NAMIBIA
BOTS
ZIM
MOZ
AUSTRALIA

SOUTH AFRICA
NEW
ZEALAND

2050
LIFE EXPECTANCY AT BIRTH
for people born in 2050
projected 1998
borders 1998

- over 83 years
- 80 to 83 years
- 75 to 79 years
- under 75 years

LIVING LONGER
Number of years of additional life expected
2050 compared with 1995

- over 20 years
- 10 to 20 years

2050
THE WIDENING GAP
Difference between life expectancy of men and women born in 2050 compared with those born in 1995
projected 1998
borders 1998

In most countries, women will continue to live longer than men.

- smaller gap
- no significant change
- greater gap

New infectious diseases are identified every two to three years. Most are caused by viruses emerging from forests and are not easily transmitted. New viruses could spread even more rapidly in the future. More people are living in crowded towns and cities, air travel is increasing, and more people are living into vulnerable old age.

Global warming will bring increases in many infectious diseases, especially those spread mainly in food or by mosquitoes: malaria, dengue, cholera and hepatitis. By 2030, when the climate may have moved 150 miles north, these tropical diseases could reach Europe (see **Global Warming**, pages 18–19).

Tuberculosis, malaria, and gonorrhea are making a comeback and are increasingly difficult to treat.

Overall, deaths from infectious disease will decline and some diseases will be eradicated. Smallpox, a centuries-old scourge, was eradicated in 1979. Other infectious diseases, such as polio, guinea worm, rubella, and mumps, should be eradicated by early in the 21st century. By then many other infections, such as leprosy and urban rabies, will probably be kept in check (although a disease found in animals can never be completely eradicated).

As yet there is no evidence that returning space explorers have brought any germs back to earth.

Sources:
see pages 122–5

CANADA
Creutzfeldt-Jakob disease (CJD) 1979

bovine spongiform encephalopathy (BSE) 1986
salmonella (new strain) 1988
UNITED KINGDOM

USA
cryptosporidiosis 1976
Legionnaires' disease 1976
new E coli (157) 1982
hepatitis C 1989

MEXICO
JAMAICA
BELIZE
HONDURAS
GUATEMALA
EL SALVADOR
NICARAGUA
COSTA RICA
PANAMA
HAITI
DOM REP
Venezuelan hemorrhagic fever 1991
VENEZUELA
TRINIDAD & TOBAGO
SURINAME
COLOMBIA
ECUADOR
PERU
BRAZIL
Brazilian hemorrhagic fever 1994
BOLIVIA
ARGENTINA

Africa AIDS 1970
SENEGAL
GUINEA-BISSAU
SIERRA LEONE
LIBERIA
GUINEA
CÔTE d'IVOIRE
GHANA
TOGO
MALI
BURKINA FASO

Ebola virus 1976

MOSQUITO BITES
Risk of contracting malaria *1990s*

In the 1990s, 45 percent of the world's population are exposed to malaria. By the 2090s this may have risen to 60 percent and include New York, Rome and Tokyo.

■ high risk

■ some risk

RUSSIA
USA
CHINA
INDIA
BRAZIL

The Atlas of the Future Copyright © Myriad Editions Limited

28

Superbugs

by 2020
INFECTIOUS DISEASES
Declining number of deaths
Numbers and percentages
of all deaths

1996
17 million 34%

2000
15 million 26%

2020
10 million 15%

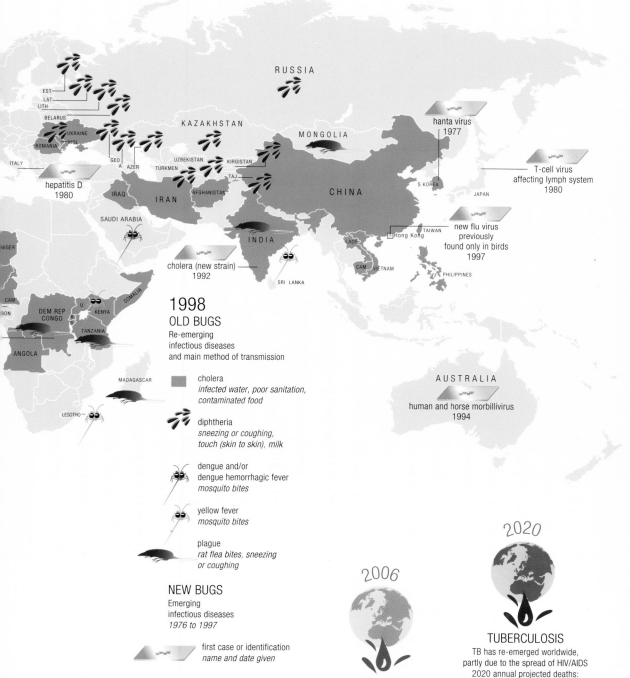

RUSSIA

KAZAKHSTAN

MONGOLIA

EST
LAT
LITH
BELARUS
UKRAINE
ROMANIA
MOL
ITALY
GEO
A
AZER
TURKMEN
UZBEKISTAN
KIRGISTAN
TAJ
AFGHANISTAN
IRAQ
IRAN

hanta virus
1977

T-cell virus
affecting lymph system
1980

hepatitis D
1980

SAUDI ARABIA

CHINA

S KOREA

JAPAN

Hong Kong
TAIWAN

new flu virus
previously
found only in birds
1997

INDIA

LAOS

cholera (new strain)
1992

SRI LANKA

CAM
VIETNAM

PHILIPPINES

NIGER

CAM
BON
DEM REP
CONGO
U
R
B
S
KENYA
SOMALIA
TANZANIA

MADAGASCAR

ANGOLA

LESOTHO

1998
OLD BUGS
Re-emerging
infectious diseases
and main method of transmission

cholera
*infected water, poor sanitation,
contaminated food*

diphtheria
*sneezing or coughing,
touch (skin to skin), milk*

**dengue and/or
dengue hemorrhagic fever**
mosquito bites

yellow fever
mosquito bites

plague
*rat flea bites, sneezing
or coughing*

NEW BUGS
Emerging
infectious diseases
1976 to 1997

first case or identification
name and date given

AUSTRALIA

human and horse morbillivirus
1994

2006

HIV/AIDS
2006 peak: 1.7 million deaths
2005 sub-Saharan Africa 800,000 deaths
2010 India 500,000 deaths

2020

TUBERCULOSIS
TB has re-emerged worldwide,
partly due to the spread of HIV/AIDS
2020 annual projected deaths:
optimistic 1.3 million
pessimistic 3.3 million

Everywhere in the world people are living longer (see **Lifetimes**, pages 26–7), which means we stand more chance of developing at least one of the diseases influenced by lifestyles. Women live longer than men and are even more likely to be affected. Diseases strongly associated with smoking, diet, exercise, and stress will probably be the leading diseases of the new century.

Diabetes is one of the most daunting challenges of the lifestyle diseases. Worldwide, the number of diabetes sufferers will more than double by 2025. The more common adult-onset diabetes is associated with lifestyle and especially with overweight. Diabetes is linked to heart disease, kidney failure, blindness, gangrene of the legs, and problems in pregnancy, especially when inadequately treated.

As a result of tobacco use, lung cancer is increasing exponentially worldwide. The tobacco epidemic will escalate, especially among women. By 2025, only 15 percent of the world's smokers will live in the rich world, and tobacco-related diseases will have moved over to the poor world.

Breast cancer is found mainly in rich countries. The rise in most cancers, other than lung and breast cancer, is mainly due to living longer.

Coronary heart disease will continue to rise in developing countries and continue to decline in both Europe and North America. More will suffer from Alzheimer's disease.

As medical skills improve, many more premature and HIV-infected infants, war casualties, and victims of accidents and violence will survive. But many may have to live with disabilities for the rest of their lives.

Sources: see pages 122–5

RISE IN LIFESTYLE DISEASES
Deaths from lifestyle diseases as proportion of all deaths *1990 and 2020*

1990

lifestyle diseases 55%

total deaths 49 million

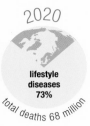

2020

lifestyle diseases 73%

total deaths 68 million

RANK ORDER OF 15 LEADING CAUSES OF DEATH AND DISABILITY
◀ *1990 compared with 2020* ▶

1990		2020
pneumonia and bronchitis	1	coronary heart disease
diarrheal diseases	2	severe depression
conditions arising around birth	3	road traffic accidents
severe depression	4	stroke
coronary heart disease	5	chronic bronchitis and emphysema
stroke	6	pneumonia and bronchitis
tuberculosis	7	tuberculosis
measles	8	war injuries
road traffic accidents	9	diarrheal diseases
defects from before birth	10	HIV
malaria	11	conditions arising around birth
chronic bronchitis	12	injuries from violence
falls	13	defects from before birth
iron-deficiency anemia	14	self-inflicted injuries
malnutrition	15	trachea, bronchus and lung cancers

DEATHS FROM SMOKING
millions

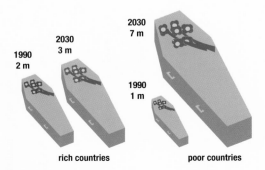

rich countries

1990
2 m

2030
3 m

poor countries

2030
7 m

1990
1 m

Lifestyle Diseases

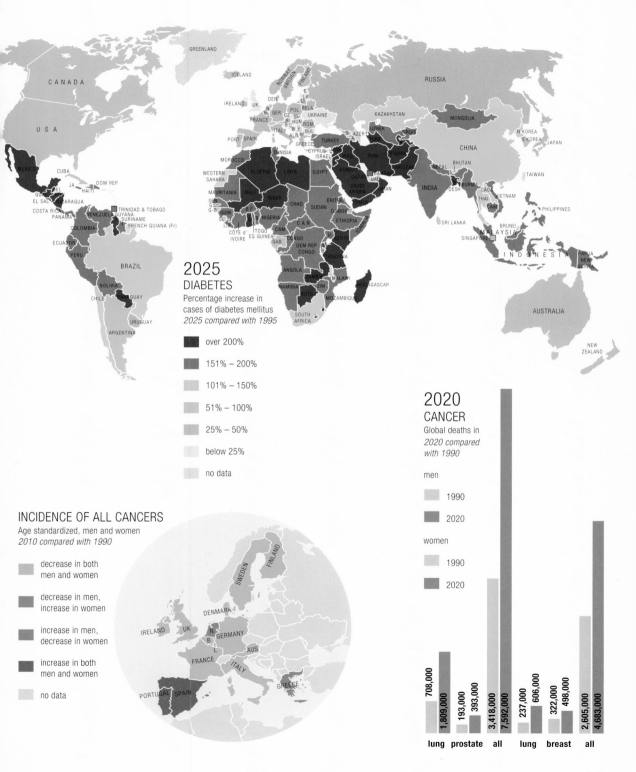

2025
DIABETES
Percentage increase in cases of diabetes mellitus
2025 compared with 1995

- over 200%
- 151% – 200%
- 101% – 150%
- 51% – 100%
- 25% – 50%
- below 25%
- no data

INCIDENCE OF ALL CANCERS
Age standardized, men and women
2010 compared with 1990

- decrease in both men and women
- decrease in men, increase in women
- increase in men, decrease in women
- increase in both men and women
- no data

2020
CANCER
Global deaths in
2020 compared with 1990

men
- 1990
- 2020

women
- 1990
- 2020

	men			women	
lung	prostate	all	lung	breast	all
708,000 / 1,809,000	193,000 / 393,000	3,418,000 / 7,592,000	237,000 / 606,000	322,000 / 498,000	2,605,000 / 4,683,000

Within the rich world there will be a shift in health care, from treatment to prevention and early detection. The focus of health care will be transferred away from hospitals and toward homes, schools, and workplaces.

Robotics and nanotechnology (see **Artificial Intelligence**, pages 36–7 and **Nanotechnology**, pages 86–7) will make surgery more minimalistic, less invasive and more remote. Hospitals will carry out less general surgery and will provide mainly transplants, replacement of body parts, and trauma care. Hospitals, surgical equipment and operating rooms will be tested in virtual reality design before they are built.

Prototypes of software to help doctors make a diagnosis and suggest appropriate treatment are already being tested successfully in the USA and UK and should be generally available before 2000.

Medical schools will teach students how to access electronic information rather than amass vast quantities of facts. They will learn anatomy from electronic medical libraries and first practice surgical procedures in virtual reality.

Developing countries will continue to rely heavily on low-tech medicine, such as immunization. But doctors and medical staff everywhere will have better access to specialist advice via low orbit satellites. Paradoxically, high-tech medicine will increase the cries for humane and caring medical treatment.

Genetic markers could be used to screen mass populations and, through diet or gene substitution, for example, largely prevent specific diseases.

Rapid advances in medical technology will raise a range of new ethical problems. Already insurance companies are demanding access to genetic tests.

Sources: see pages 122–5

late 1990s

US $20 billion

early 21st century

US $100 billion

SPENDING ON
TELEMEDICINE
in the USA

by 2006

Geneticists from around the world are working to identify all 100,000 genes in the human body by 2006. They will then map how the genes interact with one another.

The Human Genome Project will identify the roots of many genetic diseases.

Its findings will help human health through prenatal diagnosis, design of new drugs, gene therapy and, potentially, organ transplants from genetically manipulated animals.

Gene chips can already rapidly detect genes linked to HIV/AIDS and cystic fibrosis from a single drop of blood. By 2006, the Human Genome Project may be able to use the chips to see how genes interact, to improve understanding of diseases such as diabetes.

by 2020
Nanosurgeons, or submicroscopic robots, will be able to crawl through arteries. They will scrape away fatty deposits, test for toxic chemicals, hunt down cancer cells, and repair damaged or diseased parts.

Gears, motors and other microparts 50-300 microns in size have already been created. Future nanomachines will contain gears no bigger than a protein molecule.

High-Tech Health

SOME PREDICTED DEVELOPMENTS IN HEALTH CARE

- by 2010
- by 2020
- by 2030
- by 2040

DIAGNOSIS

- computer diagnosis and treatment
- computers rather than technicians scan specimens for cancer cells
- electrocardiograms, X- rays, ultrasounds, pathology slides transmitted electronically to central diagnostic centers (often in another country)
- genetic screening from mouth smear
- blood, urine and other specimens, rather than patients, transmitted to specialist centers
- injected nanomachines, too small to see under a normal microscope, scour the body to detect damaged and diseased parts

TREATMENT

- vaccines against malaria, herpes simplex, dengue, HIV/AIDS and human papilloma virus
- databases of results of clinical trials determine which treatments work, including alternative therapies
- surgeon operates by remote control of robotics at distant operating theater
- submicroscopic amounts of drugs home in to treat damaged cells but leave healthy cells unaffected
- genetic manipulation and drug treatment
- many previously untreatable diseases now curable, such as secondary cancers
- surgeons train on virtual reality surgical simulators rather than on animals and humans
- telesurgery for people exposed to high radioactivity, HIV positive, or any new highly infectious disease; or for people in remote places such as astronauts
- tiny nanomachines carry drugs or radiation to target disease within individual cells
- other treatments largely replace all except trauma surgery; remaining surgery becomes less invasive
- genetic treatment for many cancers
- genetic manipulation of gender
- computerized auto-doc externally detects and treats illness by magnetic and resonance therapy

PERSONAL

- full personal medical records stored on smart card
- individuals seek medical opinions on the internet
- home diagnostic kits for many diseases
- personal monitors connected to hospitals or commercial providers enable independence
- individual's genome part of personal medical record
- miniscule computer with microsensors automatically sensing and recording health data can be everyday wear
- instantaneous computer language translation enables patients to be understood by doctors in any country
- possible for patients' knowledge of their own health to equal that of doctors in 1990s

At the end of the twentieth century, a few people are walking around with kidneys, hearts, livers, lungs, pancreas, bone marrow, corneas or skin that started life in another human, or even an incubator.

In the mid-1990s, the global demand for transplant organs far outstrips supply, leading to a flourishing trade in organs from the poor to the rich. Fewer than a third of countries have laws forbidding the sale of human organs. Developments in cloning and artificial human parts are not sufficiently far advanced to satisfy demand.

However, over the next few decades, there will be less reliance on transplants of body parts from other humans. Factories will be developed for growing human parts. Genetically engineered transgenic pigs will be bred as donors for human organ transplants without risk of rejection. Individual body parts will be cloned, starting with blood cells and nerves. Artificial organs will become available.

By 2030, it should be possible to replace or transplant most body parts, as long as we can afford them. In theory everything will be changeable, to fit our personal needs and taste.

The ethical and social implications of some of these medical advances are enormous.

Sources: see pages 122–5

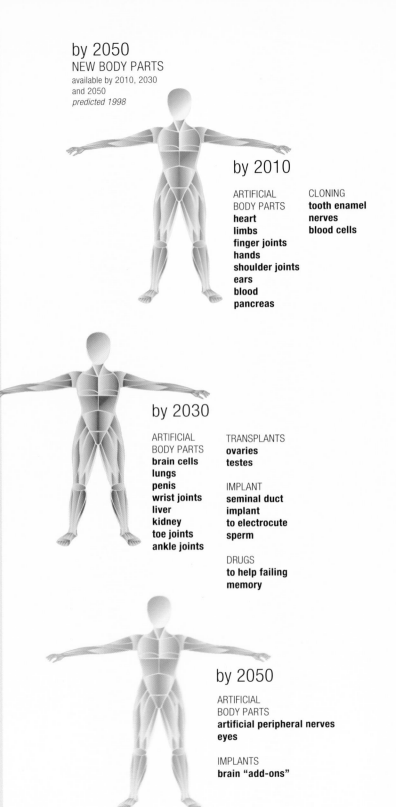

by 2050
NEW BODY PARTS
available by 2010, 2030 and 2050
predicted 1998

by 2010

ARTIFICIAL
BODY PARTS
heart
limbs
finger joints
hands
shoulder joints
ears
blood
pancreas

CLONING
tooth enamel
nerves
blood cells

by 2030

ARTIFICIAL
BODY PARTS
brain cells
lungs
penis
wrist joints
liver
kidney
toe joints
ankle joints

TRANSPLANTS
ovaries
testes

IMPLANT
seminal duct
implant
to electrocute
sperm

DRUGS
to help failing
memory

by 2050

ARTIFICIAL
BODY PARTS
artificial peripheral nerves
eyes

IMPLANTS
brain "add-ons"

Body Parts

by 2050
BODY PARTS
available mid-1990s
or predicted date available

- available mid-1990s
- available by 2010
- available by 2030
- available by 2050

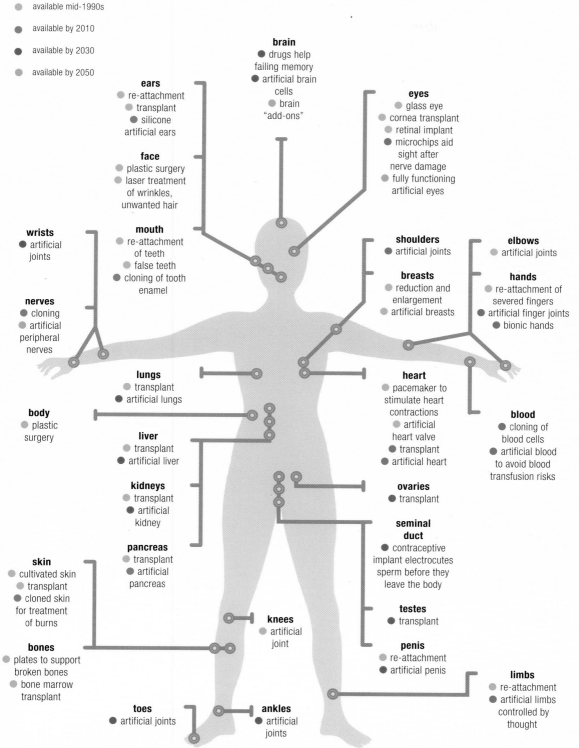

brain
- drugs help failing memory
- artificial brain cells
- brain "add-ons"

ears
- re-attachment
- transplant
- silicone artificial ears

eyes
- glass eye
- cornea transplant
- retinal implant
- microchips aid sight after nerve damage
- fully functioning artificial eyes

face
- plastic surgery
- laser treatment of wrinkles, unwanted hair

wrists
- artificial joints

mouth
- re-attachment of teeth
- false teeth
- cloning of tooth enamel

shoulders
- artificial joints

elbows
- artificial joints

breasts
- reduction and enlargement
- artificial breasts

hands
- re-attachment of severed fingers
- artificial finger joints
- bionic hands

nerves
- cloning
- artificial peripheral nerves

lungs
- transplant
- artificial lungs

heart
- pacemaker to stimulate heart contractions
- artificial heart valve
- transplant
- artificial heart

body
- plastic surgery

liver
- transplant
- artificial liver

blood
- cloning of blood cells
- artificial blood to avoid blood transfusion risks

kidneys
- transplant
- artificial kidney

ovaries
- transplant

pancreas
- transplant
- artificial pancreas

seminal duct
- contraceptive implant electrocutes sperm before they leave the body

skin
- cultivated skin
- transplant
- cloned skin for treatment of burns

knees
- artificial joint

testes
- transplant

bones
- plates to support broken bones
- bone marrow transplant

penis
- re-attachment
- artificial penis

limbs
- re-attachment
- artificial limbs controlled by thought

toes
- artificial joints

ankles
- artificial joints

35

Computers can already handle simple thought recognition, and summarize both text and abstracts automatically. Before the end of the 20th century they will be able to recognize body language and gestures. New forms of computing based on chemicals, evolved or programmed analog chips and quantum effects will vastly increase the effective power of computers in the early part of the 21st century.

Just as robots are already radically changing factories, so 21st century intelligent computers could radically change our offices.

Robotics and artificial intelligence are both sciences that developed from cybernetics. Their goal is to build autonomous machines with the intelligence of human beings. As early as 2005, robots will be able to move about on two legs. In the future, the boundaries between humans and machines could begin to blur. Artificial intelligence is already so successful that it is raising new ethical issues.

To build an artificial human it is necessary to create a robot that shows all the biological properties associated with the real thing. Can it heal itself? Does it adapt, learn and evolve? Is it intelligent? Can it communicate? Are there mechanisms, such as hormones, to maintain the long-term order of the body?

Over the next century, it may become technically possible to create androids with near human abilities.

Sources: see pages 122–5

SOME PREDICTED DEVELOPMENTS IN ARTIFICIAL INTELLIGENCE

- by 2010
- by 2020
- by 2030
- by 2040

DEVELOPMENT OF THE INTELLIGENT COMPUTER

- natural language information retrieval and interaction *1999*
- has personality *2000*
- files and retrieves documents on demand *2000*
- manages diaries and appointments *2002*
- schedules workers and resources to job *2002*
- evolves programs with 100,000 lines of code *2002*
- identifies most suitable suppliers *2005*
- manages complex finance systems *2005*
- reads, replies to, and screens email *2005*
- arranges travel *2005*
- negotiates and coordinates business functions *2007*

- programs can resist attacks by computer viruses and adapt to them *2007*
- expert systems surpass human learning and logic *2010*
- purges data automatically, keeping important items *2010*
- evolves most of own software *2010*
- summarizes multiple documents and reports on options *2010*
- summarizes staff performance and reports on options *2010*
- artificial intelligence models extensively used in business management *2010*
- screens and interviews job candidates *2015*
- understands text *2015*
- computing by wet chemical processes *2015*
- computer programs grown from seeds *2015*
- creates original text documents *2017*
- artificial brain of insect and small animal *2020*
- thought recognition used as everyday means of input *2025*
- smart computer provides transparent interface to humans *2025*
- text creativity comparable to that of humans *2025*

36

Artificial Intelligence

DEVELOPMENT OF THE INTELLIGENT ROBOT

- tactile sensors comparable to human touch *2004*
- computers recognize facial expressions *2005*
- full voice interaction with machine *2005*
- voice synthesis comparable to human voice *2005*
- self-healing computer programs *2005*
- computers use hormone-like control *2005*
- computers evolve own hardware structure *2005*
- robot walks on two legs on rough terrain *2005*
- computers speak to each other in natural language *2006*
- self-organizing adaptive integrated circuits *2007*
- reasoning with complex, noisy and uncertain information *2010*
- systems continuously evolve and update *2010*

- translation device makes simple conversation *2010*
- behavior-based computers as complex as dog or cat *2010*
- flavor and odor sensors comparable to human taste and smell *2010*
- robots seek out own multisource power supply *2010*
- machine use of human-like memorizing, recognition, learning *2012*
- behavior-based computers as complex as humans *2012*
- able to use reasoning by analogy comparable to humans *2015*
- computer vision comparable to human vision *2015*
- computers with human-like emotions *2015*
- flavor and odor sensors comparable to dog's taste and smell *2015*
- intelligent materials with sensors, storage, and effectors *2015*
- self-diagnostic, self-repairing robots *2017*
- artificial brain of insect or small animal *2020*
- artificial brain *2035*

TOWARD THE ANDROID

- polymer gels for muscles, bioreactors, information processing *2010*
- artificial cell membranes with active transport and receptors *2017*
- smart skin for intelligent clothing and direct repair by machine *2020*

MAIN CENTERS OF ROBOTICS AND ARTIFICIAL INTELLIGENCE
late 1990s

London

Moscow

Silicon Valley

New York

Tokyo

Infertility is a global problem. It affects between 50 to 80 million people worldwide, or 8 to 12 percent of couples.

There will be a growing demand for infertility treatment as more and more women delay childbirth. As education and prosperity increase, this trend will continue worldwide.

Infertility treatments will be limited less by technology than what societies will tolerate. Different treatments will be available in different countries, as some, such as Germany, pursue ethically conservative policies while others, such as Italy and the UK, are more liberal.

New technologies may make infertility treatments safer for women. Fewer embryos will be implanted, and the risks associated with multiple births reduced, if the chances of successful pregnancies and live births improve.

As treatments for male infertility become more sophisticated, the use of donor insemination will be less popular. But new treatments to help "weak" sperm may be restricted if rates of fetal abnormality increase.

Worldwide, sexually transmitted diseases, such as chlamydia and gonorrhea, are a common cause of infertility. In developing countries especially, health education and early treatment will have a far greater impact on infertility than expensive new technologies.

Sources: see pages 122–5

by 2010
DESIGNER BABIES

Fertilized embryos may be screened for genetic disorders before being implanted. Screening can determine gender, the risk of certain cancers, and illnesses, such as Tay-Sachs disease and cystic fibrosis. Already genes for a range of other traits – from premature baldness to eye color – have been located. Scientists expect to locate the myopia gene by 2000.

Controversial developments include:

 Eggs from aborted fetuses implanted in women with damaged or missing ovaries.

Embryo splitting to allow identical twins to be born several years apart.

Egg donation for postmenopausal women.

Preserving sperm to achieve posthumous pregnancy.

Increasing surrogacy with or without payment.

 Extending permissible storage time for embryos.

New Conceptions

INFERTILITY

Women who have never conceived despite cohabitation and exposure to pregnancy for two years
1991 percentages of all women

- 15% and over
- 10% – 14%
- 5% – 9%
- under 5%
- no data

by 2000
REPRODUCTIVE TECHNOLOGIES

WOMEN
- Immature oocyte retrieval collects immature eggs from the ovary to mature in vitro, avoiding the use of stimulatory hormones.

- Embryo micromanipulation, or assisted hatching, makes a hole in the outer skin of the egg capsule, helping the fertilized embryo to emerge and implant successfully.

MEN
- Intracytoplasmic sperm injection (ICSI) injects a sperm directly into an egg cell, enabling men with a low sperm count to take part in *in vitro* fertilization (IVF).

- Subzonal insemination (SUZI), compensates for a defective sperm's inability to penetrate the egg's outer shell by depositing it below the egg's protein capsule.

- Immature sperm may be extracted from the testes and treated to improve their ability to fertilize an egg.

The Future of
Resources

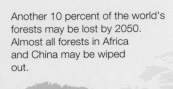

Another 10 percent of the world's forests may be lost by 2050. Almost all forests in Africa and China may be wiped out.

There is danger of severe loss in South East Asia and South America. Old undisturbed forest is in decline everywhere.

Most loss will be caused by logging, mining, the development of energy, farming, roadbuilding, and pollution. Given climate change in the USA, it could be caused by a shift eastward in the agricultural land of the midwest.

Russia is opening up large tracts of untouched temperate forest and Siberian boreal forest to logging companies from the USA, Europe, Japan and South Korea.

Frontier forests are complete ecosystems that provide safe havens for whole arrays of indigenous species. Tropical forests provide habitat for about half the world's animal and bird species (see also **Biodiversity**, pages 44–5).

Humans have always plundered forests rather than preserve them. Tropical forest is at risk of being bulldozed out of existence. During the 1980s alone, 8 percent of the world's tropical forest was lost, and there have been further losses in the 1990s.

Sources: see pages 122–5

TOTAL FORESTS
mid 1990s
thousand sq km

World total: 33.4 m sq km

N America 8,483
Russia 8,083
S America 6,800
Asia 4,275
Africa 2,302
Europe 1,521
C America 970
Oceania 929

Forests

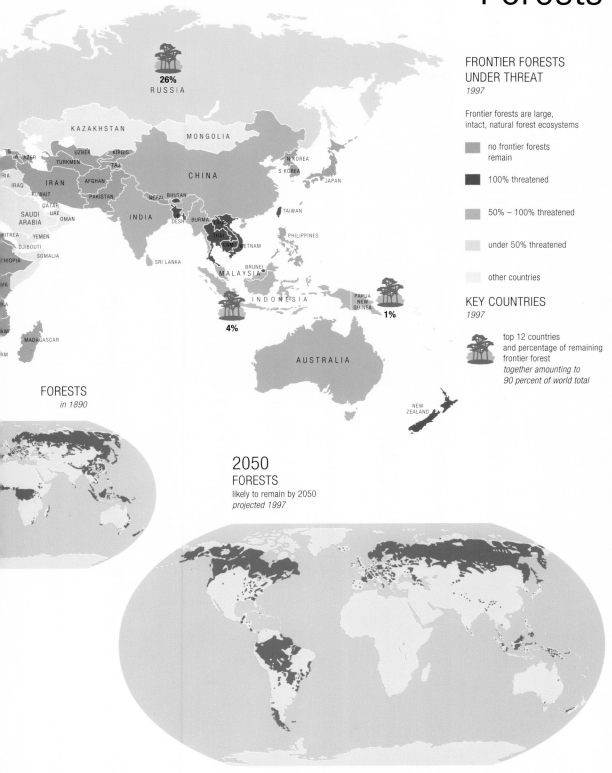

FRONTIER FORESTS UNDER THREAT
1997

Frontier forests are large, intact, natural forest ecosystems

- no frontier forests remain
- 100% threatened
- 50% – 100% threatened
- under 50% threatened
- other countries

KEY COUNTRIES
1997

top 12 countries and percentage of remaining frontier forest *together amounting to 90 percent of world total*

26% RUSSIA

4%

1%

RA AZER
TURKMEN
UZBEK
KIRGIS
TAJ
KAZAKHSTAN
MONGOLIA
IRAN
AFGHAN
IRAQ
KUWAIT
QATAR
UAE
PAKISTAN
CHINA
N KOREA
S KOREA
JAPAN
SAUDI ARABIA
OMAN
NEPAL
BHUTAN
INDIA
DESH
BURMA
TAIWAN
RITREA
YEMEN
DJIBOUTI
HIOPIA
SOMALIA
SRI LANKA
THAI
CAM
VIETNAM
PHILIPPINES
YA
MALAYSIA
BRUNEI
MADAGASCAR
AM
INDONESIA
PAPUA NEW GUINEA
AUSTRALIA
NEW ZEALAND

FORESTS
in 1890

2050
FORESTS
likely to remain by 2050
projected 1997

About 1.7 million species have so far been identified, out of a world total of perhaps 14 million, of which most are insects. Some estimates put the number of species at over 100 million.

During the 1990s, millions of mysterious new species have been found living in ultra rich ecosystems, down near the floor of the deep oceans.

Between 5 and 20 percent of some plant and mammal species will become extinct within decades. Hunting and poaching, whether for livelihood or profit, will continue to take their toll. Loss of habitat is the biggest single cause. Rich coastal ecosystems are particularly vulnerable to the outward spread of cities and ports.

Designated protected areas help to conserve species. Whole ecosystems must be preserved in order to maintain the natural balance necessary for the survival of diverse species.

Human survival depends upon biodiversity. The natural world provides ingredients and materials for foods, medicines, cosmetics, fuels, and legions of household and industrial products.

In the future, it will be possible to monitor the earth's last remaining wetlands, mangrove swamps, or tropical forests via satellites and the internet, without the damage caused by human intervention.

Sources: see pages 122–5

TOTAL KNOWN SPECIES
mid 1990s

270,000

9,672 plants
6,900 birds
4,400 reptiles
4,327 amphibians
mammals

4,036
101
70 USA

12,500
140
89 MEXICO

62

4,000 ECUADOR
COLOMBIA

8,000

VENEZUELA

5,356
45
109 PERU
BOLIVIA

96
177 BRAZIL

4,000 ARGENTINA

47

Biodiversity

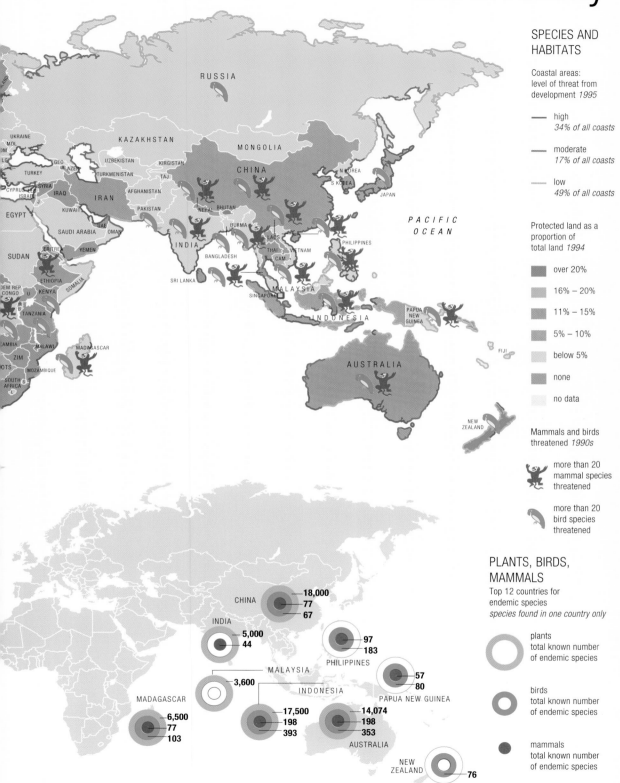

SPECIES AND HABITATS

Coastal areas:
level of threat from
development *1995*

— high
34% of all coasts

— moderate
17% of all coasts

— low
49% of all coasts

Protected land as a
proportion of
total land *1994*

- over 20%
- 16% – 20%
- 11% – 15%
- 5% – 10%
- below 5%
- none
- no data

Mammals and birds
threatened *1990s*

more than 20
mammal species
threatened

more than 20
bird species
threatened

PLANTS, BIRDS, MAMMALS

Top 12 countries for
endemic species
species found in one country only

plants
total known number
of endemic species

birds
total known number
of endemic species

mammals
total known number
of endemic species

CHINA
18,000
77
67

INDIA
5,000
44

PHILIPPINES
97
183

MALAYSIA
3,600

INDONESIA
17,500
198
393

PAPUA NEW GUINEA
57
80

MADAGASCAR
6,500
77
103

AUSTRALIA
14,074
198
353

NEW ZEALAND
76

45

Fresh water is abundant globally but scarce locally. The world's supply of renewable fresh water could meet the demands of a growing population if supplies were distributed evenly. In addition to national water scarcity and stress, water is poorly distributed across regions within countries and across seasons. The drier regions of many countries that have sufficient water overall, such as the USA, will continue to experience periodic water shortages.

In 2050, two billion people could be living in water-stressed or water-scarce countries. For many countries, inadequate supplies of fresh water will impede economic development and create further tension between states competing for shared water resources.

In developing countries, the increased demand for domestic and industrial water is expected to exceed the increased demand for agricultural water. Coupled with escalating costs of developing new water resources, this new trend could threaten future food production (see **Food**, pages 48–9), especially if the need for household and industrial water is met by draining agriculture's share.

Sources: see pages 122–5

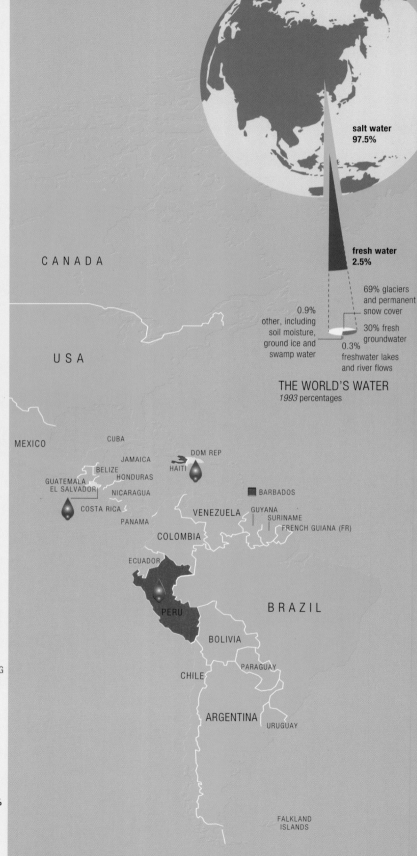

salt water
97.5%

fresh water
2.5%

0.9%
other, including
soil moisture,
ground ice and
swamp water

69% glaciers
and permanent
snow cover

30% fresh
groundwater

0.3%
freshwater lakes
and river flows

THE WORLD'S WATER
1993 percentages

CANADA

USA

MEXICO

CUBA

JAMAICA

BELIZE

HONDURAS

GUATEMALA
EL SALVADOR

NICARAGUA

COSTA RICA

PANAMA

DOM REP

HAITI

BARBADOS

VENEZUELA

GUYANA

SURINAME

FRENCH GUIANA (FR)

COLOMBIA

ECUADOR

PERU

BRAZIL

BOLIVIA

CHILE

PARAGUAY

ARGENTINA

URUGUAY

FALKLAND
ISLANDS

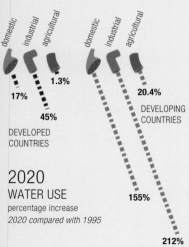

domestic   industrial   agricultural

domestic   industrial   agricultural

1.3%

17%

45%

20.4%

DEVELOPED
COUNTRIES

DEVELOPING
COUNTRIES

2020
WATER USE
percentage increase
2020 compared with 1995

155%

212%

Water

1995

relative sufficiency **92%**

stress **5%**
scarcity **3%**

world population 5.7 billion

2050

scarcity 18%
relative sufficiency 58%
stress 24%

world population 9.4 billion

WATER SHORTAGES
Proportion of world's population
facing water shortages
1995 and *2050*

ICELAND

NORWAY   SWEDEN   FINLAND

RUSSIA

DENMARK   EST   LAT   LITH

IRELAND   UK   NETH   GERMANY   POLAND   KAZAKHSTAN   MONGOLIA
BEL   L   CZECH   SLO   UKRAINE
S   AUS   HUNG   MOL
FRANCE   S   C   B-H YUG   ROMANIA   UZBEKISTAN   KIRGISTAN   CHINA
ITALY   ALB   M   BULG   TAJ
PORTUGAL   SPAIN   GREECE   TURKEY   GEORGIA   AZER   TURKMENISTAN   AFGHANISTAN   NEPAL   BHUTAN
MALTA   CYPRUS   LEB   SYRIA   IRAQ   IRAN   PAKISTAN   B
TUNISIA   ISRAEL   JOR   DESH   INDIA

MOROCCO   KUWAIT   BAHRAIN   QATAR
WESTERN   ALGERIA   LIBYA   EGYPT   SAUDI   UAE   SRI LANKA
SAHARA   ARABIA   OMAN
MAURITANIA   MALI   NIGER   CHAD   SUDAN   ERITREA   YEMEN
APE VERDE   BURKINA   NIGERIA   DJIBOUTI
SENEGAL   FASO   CAR   ETHIOPIA
GAMBIA   GUINEA   BENIN   CAMEROON   SOMALIA
INEA-BISSAU   GHANA   EQ GUINEA   CONGO   KENYA
SIERRA LEONE   CÔTE d'   TOGO   GABON
LIBERIA   IVOIRE   DEM REP   COMOROS
CONGO   TANZANIA

2050
FRESH WATER
Availability per person per year
cubic meters
projected 1997
borders 1998

ANGOLA   MALAWI   MAURITIUS
ZAMBIA   MADAGASCAR
NAMIBIA   ZIM   MOZAMBIQUE
BOTS
SOUTH   S
AFRICA

■ water scarcity:
under 1,000 cubic meters
per person
*chronic water shortages impede
economic development and cause
environmental degradation*

□ water stress:
1,000-1,700 cubic meters
per person
*chronic and widespread
water supply problems*

□ relative water sufficiency:
over 1,700 cubic meters
per person
intermittent or localized shortages

💧 relative sufficiency in 1995
although shortage predicted
for 2050

Note: Based on
UN population data 1996

47

World food supplies will continue to rise but many poor will still go hungry. In sub-Saharan Africa, the number of malnourished children is expected to rise by a further 14 million as growth in incomes will barely exceed population growth. South Asia will be better off, but some 70 million will still be malnourished in 2020.

World trade in food will expand rapidly by 2020, driven by the needs of the developing world to import more basic staple foods.

In the future, as incomes rise and more people live in cities, more rice and wheat will be consumed, and less maize and coarse grains. Eventually there will be a further shift from rice to wheat. By 2020, people will eat more meat, especially in Asia, with the result that more cereals, particularly maize, will be fed to animals.

Crop yield growth is expected to continue to decline. Heavy use of agricultural chemicals in some regions is having an adverse impact on the environment. Water scarcity may be the biggest single threat to crop yield growth (see **Water**, pages 46–7.)

The increasing demand for food is encouraging radical developments in biotechnology and the genetic manipulation of food crops. Most developments are intended to protect plants from pests and diseases and to improve production, though the long-term effects are still unknown.

Some fruits and vegetables may soon be genetically modified to protect humans from specific diseases: grapes that reduce the risk of heart disease, or bananas containing hepatitis B vaccine. Animals may soon be genetically redesigned to produce more meat, wool, eggs, or milk.

Sources: see pages 122–5

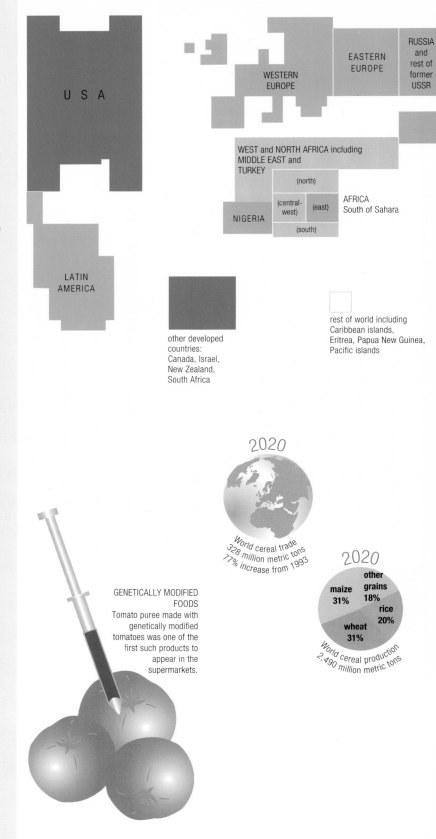

USA

WESTERN EUROPE

EASTERN EUROPE

RUSSIA and rest of former USSR

WEST and NORTH AFRICA including MIDDLE EAST and TURKEY

(north)

(central-west)

(east)

(south)

NIGERIA

AFRICA South of Sahara

LATIN AMERICA

other developed countries: Canada, Israel, New Zealand, South Africa

rest of world including Caribbean islands, Eritrea, Papua New Guinea, Pacific islands

2020

World cereal trade 328 million metric tons 77% increase from 1993

2020

maize 31%

other grains 18%

rice 20%

wheat 31%

World cereal production 2,490 million metric tons

GENETICALLY MODIFIED FOODS
Tomato puree made with genetically modified tomatoes was one of the first such products to appear in the supermarkets.

Food

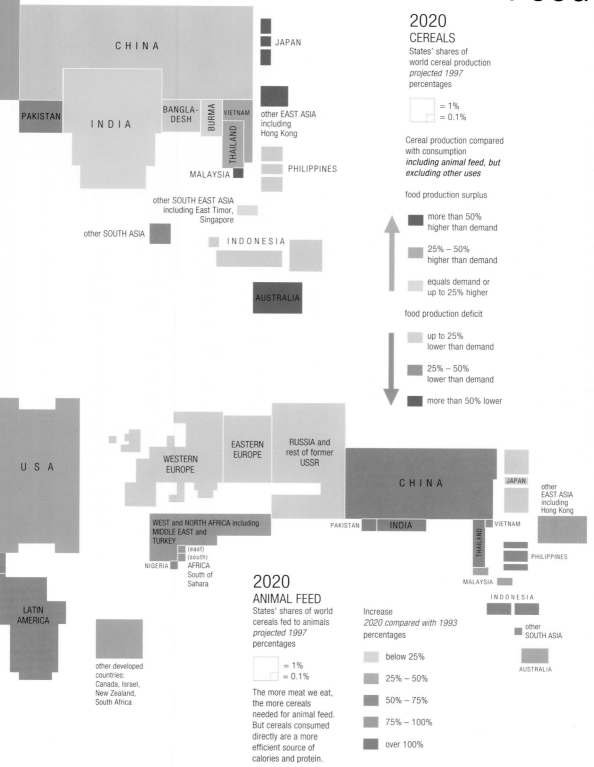

2020 CEREALS

States' shares of world cereal production *projected 1997* percentages

☐ = 1%
▫ = 0.1%

Cereal production compared with consumption *including animal feed, but excluding other uses*

food production surplus

■ more than 50% higher than demand

■ 25% – 50% higher than demand

☐ equals demand or up to 25% higher

food production deficit

☐ up to 25% lower than demand

■ 25% – 50% lower than demand

■ more than 50% lower

CHINA

JAPAN

PAKISTAN

INDIA

BANGLA-DESH

BURMA

VIETNAM

THAILAND

other EAST ASIA including Hong Kong

MALAYSIA

PHILIPPINES

other SOUTH EAST ASIA including East Timor, Singapore

other SOUTH ASIA

INDONESIA

AUSTRALIA

2020 ANIMAL FEED

States' shares of world cereals fed to animals *projected 1997* percentages

☐ = 1%
▫ = 0.1%

The more meat we eat, the more cereals needed for animal feed. But cereals consumed directly are a more efficient source of calories and protein.

Increase *2020 compared with 1993* percentages

☐ below 25%

☐ 25% – 50%

■ 50% – 75%

■ 75% – 100%

■ over 100%

USA

WESTERN EUROPE

EASTERN EUROPE

RUSSIA and rest of former USSR

CHINA

JAPAN

other EAST ASIA including Hong Kong

WEST and NORTH AFRICA including MIDDLE EAST and TURKEY

PAKISTAN

INDIA

VIETNAM

THAILAND

NIGERIA

(east)
(south)
AFRICA South of Sahara

PHILIPPINES

MALAYSIA

INDONESIA

LATIN AMERICA

other SOUTH ASIA

other developed countries: Canada, Israel, New Zealand, South Africa

AUSTRALIA

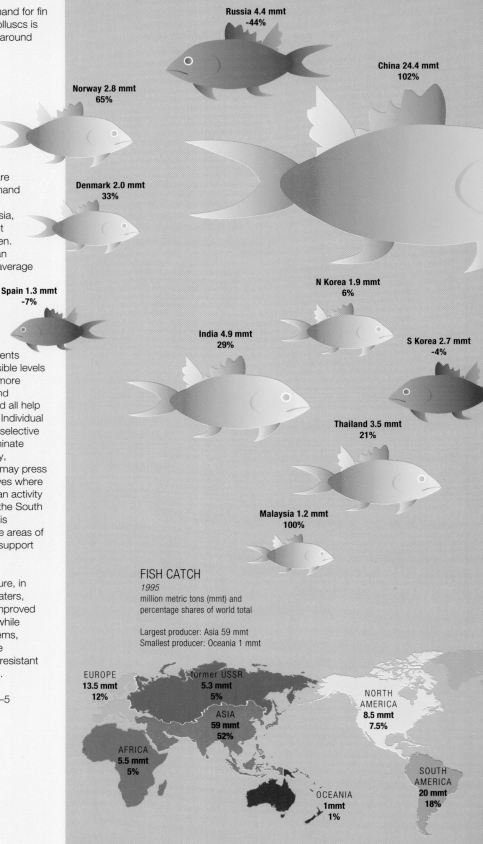

By 2010, worldwide demand for fin fish, crustaceans and molluscs is expected to increase by around 33 percent.

Iceland 1.6 mmt
7%

Norway 2.8 mmt
65%

Russia 4.4 mmt
-44%

China 24.4 mmt
102%

Denmark 2.0 mmt
33%

More and more people are eating fish, although demand varies widely country to country. In South East Asia, fish makes up 75 percent of the animal protein eaten. In Argentina, it is less than 4 percent. Globally, the average is 18 percent.

Spain 1.3 mmt
-7%

N Korea 1.9 mmt
6%

India 4.9 mmt
29%

S Korea 2.7 mmt
-4%

Since the mid-1990s, conservation measures have helped to rebuild overfished areas. Accurate stock assessments to determine the permissible levels of catch, DNA analysis, more sophisticated tagging, and acoustic censuses should all help to achieve sustainability. Individual vessel quotas and more selective nets will reduce indiscriminate fishing. More dramatically, environmental scientists may press for massive ocean reserves where virtually all forms of human activity are suspended. Around the South Pacific islands, research is underway to fertilize huge areas of unproductive oceans to support new fish populations.

Thailand 3.5 mmt
21%

Malaysia 1.2 mmt
100%

In conventional aquaculture, in both fresh and marine waters, selective breeding and improved feeds will increase yield while better quality water systems, pharmaceuticals, and the development of disease-resistant strains will reduce losses.

Sources: see pages 122–5

FISH CATCH
1995
million metric tons (mmt) and percentage shares of world total

Largest producer: Asia 59 mmt
Smallest producer: Oceania 1 mmt

EUROPE
13.5 mmt
12%

former USSR
5.3 mmt
5%

NORTH AMERICA
8.5 mmt
7.5%

ASIA
59 mmt
52%

AFRICA
5.5 mmt
5%

OCEANIA
1mmt
1%

SOUTH AMERICA
20 mmt
18%

Fishing

2010
Global fish catch 140–50 mmt
compared with 112 mmt in 1995

LEADING FISHING COUNTRIES
1995
sized in million metric tons (mmt)

 = 1 mmt

CHANGE IN FISH CATCH
1995 compared with 1990

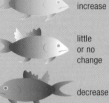 increase

little or no change

decrease

Largest increase: China 102%
Largest decrease: Russia -44%

Japan 6.8 mmt
-35%

USA 5.6 mmt
-5%

Mexico 1.4 mmt

Taiwan 1.3 mmt
-7%

Peru 8.9 mmt
29%

Vietnam 1.2 mmt
20%

Philippines 2.7 mmt
23%

Chile 7.6 mmt
32%

Indonesia 4.1 mmt
37%

40%
of fisheries
are developing

35%
of fisheries
are declining

25%
of fisheries
are mature

STATE OF THE WORLD'S FISHERIES
1995
percentages

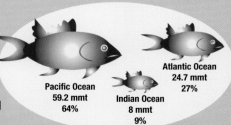

OCEAN'S SHARE OF TOTAL CATCH
1995
million metric tons (mmt)

Pacific Ocean
59.2 mmt
64%

Indian Ocean
8 mmt
9%

Atlantic Ocean
24.7 mmt
27%

51

Every region of the world will use more energy in 2010 than in the 1990s if present trends continue. Globally, the average increase is expected to be 46 percent. Industrialized countries will use four to five times more energy than developing countries.

Energy use in East and South Asia is likely to double as these regions become more industrialized. But even in developed regions, such as Western Europe and North America, an increase of

up to 25 percent is predicted.

Energy intensity – the relationship between economic performance and energy use – also differs between regions. Most developing countries will use twice as much energy as industrialized countries to produce the same amount of wealth. Becoming more efficient will help to stop further environmental damage and climate change (see **Global Warming**, pages 18–19), as will using more renewable energy and less oil and coal.

Gas is a cleaner alternative to oil and coal, and less damaging to the atmosphere. Central Eastern Europe and the Commonwealth of Independent States are expected to achieve the greatest oil and coal reductions. The Asia Pacific region will account for half the increased use of nuclear power. Industrialized countries are expected to promote the use of renewable fuels.

Sources: see pages 122–5

NORTH AMERICA

2010
+25.5%

1993

2020
+20.2%

1990

WESTERN E

AFRICA

SOUTH AND CENTRAL AMERICA

2010
+66.9%

1993

2010
ENERGY USE
by region *projected 1996*
toe (tons of oil equivalent)
per person

World average: 1.7 toe

- 5 toe and over
- 2 to 4 toe
- 1 to 2 toe
- under 1 toe

CHANGES IN ENERGY USE
2010 projection compared with 1993

World average: 46% increase

- renewable fuel
  including geothermal, hydro, energy crops, solar, wind, charcoal and wood
- oil and coal
- gas
- nuclear energy

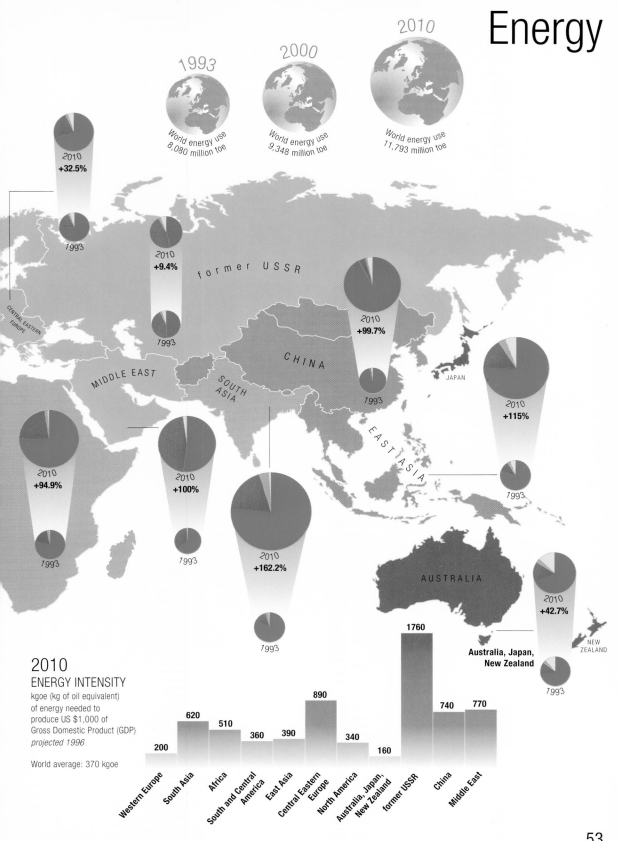

Energy

1993 — World energy use 8,080 million toe

2000 — World energy use 9,348 million toe

2010 — World energy use 11,793 million toe

CENTRAL EASTERN EUROPE — 2010 **+32.5%** / 1993

former USSR — 2010 **+9.4%** / 1993

CHINA — 2010 **+99.7%** / 1993

MIDDLE EAST — 2010 **+94.9%** / 1993

SOUTH ASIA — 2010 **+100%** / 1993

2010 **+162.2%** / 1993

EAST ASIA — 2010 **+115%** / 1993

JAPAN

AUSTRALIA

Australia, Japan, New Zealand — 2010 **+42.7%** / 1993

NEW ZEALAND

2010
ENERGY INTENSITY
kgoe (kg of oil equivalent) of energy needed to produce US $1,000 of Gross Domestic Product (GDP)
projected 1996

World average: 370 kgoe

Region	kgoe
Western Europe	200
South Asia	620
Africa	510
South and Central America	360
East Asia	390
Central Eastern Europe	890
North America	340
Australia, Japan, New Zealand	160
former USSR	1760
China	740
Middle East	770

The Future of
Communications

Information technology is transforming the global economy. With a telephone and a computer, anyone can receive and transmit data, log onto the internet (see **The Internet**, pages 58–9), communicate across the world and be part of the new information age.

Yet traditional underground cabling is expensive and in the late 1990s, three-quarters of the world's telephones are in a mere eight industrialized countries. Being able to afford a telephone is only half the battle. Getting connected can take as long as 9 years in Palestine, 20 years in Uganda, or even 40 in Tanzania.

Early in the next century vast new global undersea cabling networks will bring down the cost of international communications. New satellite systems will offer universal telephone access via mobile phones anywhere on the globe.

In their early years satellite communications will be expensive. Inmarsat is setting up community telephone booths for a few remote places in India but for a while the gap between the information-rich and the information-poor will get wider.

Computer capacity is increasing so rapidly that telecommunications networks are caught in a constant struggle to keep up. The computer will become ever more powerful and ubiquitous, so this gap will continue for some years.

Sources: see pages 122–5

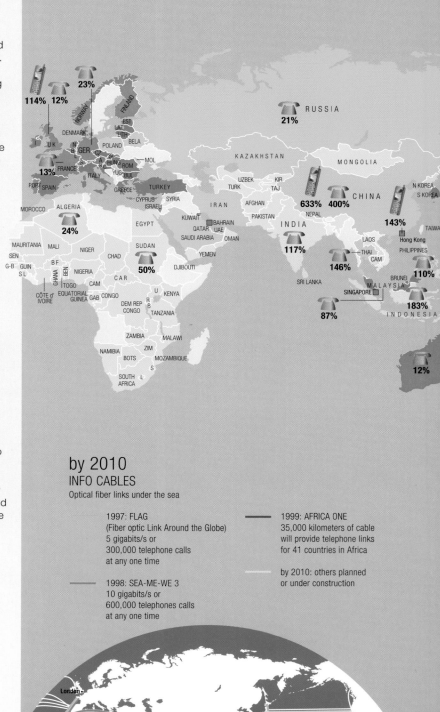

by 2010
INFO CABLES
Optical fiber links under the sea

1997: FLAG
(Fiber optic Link Around the Globe)
5 gigabits/s or
300,000 telephone calls
at any one time

1998: SEA-ME-WE 3
10 gigabits/s or
600,000 telephones calls
at any one time

1999: AFRICA ONE
35,000 kilometers of cable
will provide telephone links
for 41 countries in Africa

by 2010: others planned
or under construction

original optical
fiber cables
up to 5 gigabits/s
or 300,000
telephone calls
at any one time

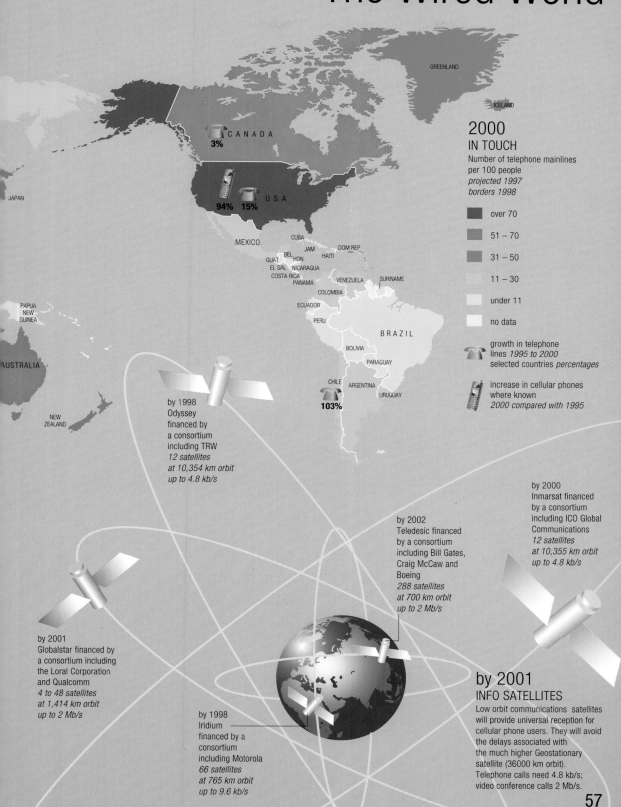

The Wired World

GREENLAND

ICELAND

CANADA
3%

JAPAN

USA
94% **15%**

MEXICO

CUBA
JAM
DOM REP
BEL
HON
HAITI
GUAT
EL SAL. NICARAGUA
COSTA RICA
PANAMA
VENEZUELA
SURINAME
COLOMBIA
ECUADOR
PERU
BRAZIL
BOLIVIA
PARAGUAY
CHILE
ARGENTINA
103%
URUGUAY

PAPUA
NEW
GUINEA

AUSTRALIA

NEW
ZEALAND

2000
IN TOUCH
Number of telephone mainlines
per 100 people
projected 1997
borders 1998

- over 70
- 51 – 70
- 31 – 50
- 11 – 30
- under 11
- no data

growth in telephone
lines *1995 to 2000*
selected countries *percentages*

increase in cellular phones
where known
2000 compared with 1995

by 1998
Odyssey
financed by
a consortium
including TRW
12 satellites
at 10,354 km orbit
up to 4.8 kb/s

by 2000
Inmarsat financed
by a consortium
including ICO Global
Communications
12 satellites
at 10,355 km orbit
up to 4.8 kb/s

by 2002
Teledesic financed
by a consortium
including Bill Gates,
Craig McCaw and
Boeing
288 satellites
at 700 km orbit
up to 2 Mb/s

by 2001
Globalstar financed by
a consortium including
the Loral Corporation
and Qualcomm
4 to 48 satellites
at 1,414 km orbit
up to 2 Mb/s

by 1998
Iridium
financed by a
consortium
including Motorola
66 satellites
at 765 km orbit
up to 9.6 kb/s

by 2001
INFO SATELLITES
Low orbit communications satellites
will provide universal reception for
cellular phone users. They will avoid
the delays associated with
the much higher Geostationary
satellite (36000 km orbit).
Telephone calls need 4.8 kb/s;
video conference calls 2 Mb/s.

57

The internet is changing so rapidly that refined projections are generally shunned. As the internet grows, it will be better organized and monitored. It will also offer more visual services and become more international. However, most services envisaged already exist on the internet in embryonic form, for the cost of a local phone call.

Education and medical care will not be restricted by geography or national borders. Through the internet It will be possible for teachers and doctors effectively to be present anywhere on the planet.

Banking, travel, and shopping services will grow rapidly. Artificially intelligent agents will gather and sift information for consumers, organize their schedules, and negotiate the best deals.

People will meet new and old friends and interact with them in virtual spaces, eventually with language translation built in. The network will put us in touch with a multitude of others with whom we share something, a way of life, common values, or common interest. But we will not always be sure whether the person we have just met is real or fictitious. Tricks and hoaxes will always be possible.

News, radio and television, and many other forms of information will increasingly be delivered in channels and broadcast by push technology on the internet. The internet may become the natural point through which all media networks converge, providing a single point of access.

By the year 2000, only a small proportion of the world's population will have their own personal computer. But over the following 20 years new technologies will change this.

Sources: see pages 122–5

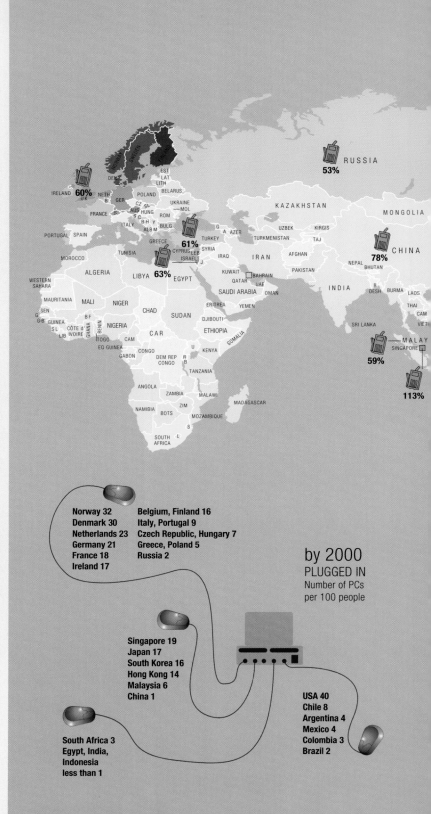

by 2000
PLUGGED IN
Number of PCs
per 100 people

Norway 32
Denmark 30
Netherlands 23
Germany 21
France 18
Ireland 17

Belgium, Finland 16
Italy, Portugal 9
Czech Republic, Hungary 7
Greece, Poland 5
Russia 2

Singapore 19
Japan 17
South Korea 16
Hong Kong 14
Malaysia 6
China 1

USA 40
Chile 8
Argentina 4
Mexico 4
Colombia 3
Brazil 2

South Africa 3
Egypt, India,
Indonesia
less than 1

The Internet

Each year the internet doubles in size. By 2001, there will be over 600 million users.

GREENLAND

CANADA

USA

BERMUDA

MEXICO   CUBA   BAHAMAS
                     DOM REP
          JA
      BEL HONDURAS HAITI
GUAT   NICARAGUA
EL SALVADOR
      COSTA RICA   TRINIDAD & TOBAGO
        PANAMA   VENEZUELA GUYANA
                            SURINAME
                   COLOMBIA FRENCH GUIANA (FR)

          ECUADOR

PERU   BRAZIL

          BOLIVIA

CHILE   PARA

100%   URUGUAY
ARGENTINA

N KOREA
S KOREA
          JAPAN
116%
   TAIWAN
g Kong   **52%**

PACIFIC
OCEAN

PHILIPPINES

DONESIA   PAPUA
           NEW
           GUINEA

AUSTRALIA

NEW
ZEALAND
        84%

COMPUTERS CONNECTED TO THE INTERNET
per 100,000 people
July 1997

- over 5000
- 3000 – 5000
- 1000 – 3000
- 500 – 1000
- 250 – 500
- 50 – 250
- below 50
- none or no data

over 50 percent increase in countries with more than 20,000 *January-July 1997*

INTERNET USERS
Share of total number of *July 1997*

world total: 74 million

= 1%
= 0.1%

EUROPE
15 million
20.3%

ASIA/PACIFIC
13 million
17.6%

AFRICA
1 million
1.3%

MIDDLE EAST
1 million
1.3%

NORTH
AMERICA
42 million
56.8%

SOUTH AMERICA
2 million
2.7%

Television will become increasingly interactive and, as a result of the spread of cable and satellite delivery systems, will offer a wealth of viewing choices for those who can afford it. The price of multichannel TV may be that we have to pay for what we watch, as and when we do so.

Digitalization, which is at the center of these changes, brings with it the capacity to transmit huge amounts of data, words, sounds, and images to television receivers in private homes. Digital television will enable viewers to select and edit programs, change camera angles, order videos, and access the internet for home shopping, music online, as well as travel and financial services.

In the short term, the digital revolution offers little to those people who are still without significant access to basic television – most of the world's population. But, in theory, the low cost of information technology should enable poor countries to leapfrog industrial technology and join a global electronic culture.

Sources: see pages 122–5

NORWAY
FINLAND
SWEDEN
ESTONIA
DENMARK
LATVIA
LITHUANIA
IRELAND
BELARUS
UK
NETH
GERMANY
POLAND
BEL
CZECH REP
UKRAINE
SLOVAK
SWITZ
AUSTRIA
HUNGARY
MOLDOVA
FRANCE
SLO
CROATIA
ROMANIA
ITALY
B - H
YUG
BULGARIA
PORTUGAL
ALB
M
SPAIN
GREECE

USA
CUBA
DOM REP
JAMAICA
MEXICO
BELIZE
HAITI
PUERTO RICO
HONDURAS
GUATEMALA
EL SALVADOR
NICARAGUA
TRINIDAD
COSTA RICA
VENEZUELA
GUYANA
PANAMA
SURINAME
FRENCH GUIANA (FR)
COLOMBIA
ECUADOR
BRAZIL
PERU
BOLIVIA
PARAGUAY
CHILE
ARGENTINA
URUGUAY

2005
MULTICHANNEL TV

in Europe
Multichannel TV households
as a proportion of all TV households
projected 1997 percentages

- over 80%
- 40% – 79%
- under 40%
- no data
- over 100% increase since 1995

in Latin America
Multichannel TV subscribers
projected 1997

- over 5 million
- 1 million – 5 million
- under 1 million
- over 100% increase since 1995

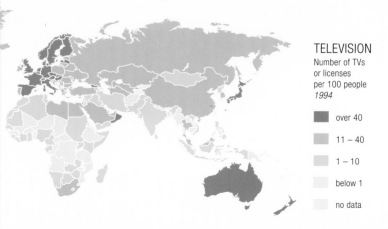

TELEVISION

Number of TVs
or licenses
per 100 people
1994

- over 40
- 11 – 40
- 1 – 10
- below 1
- no data

Media

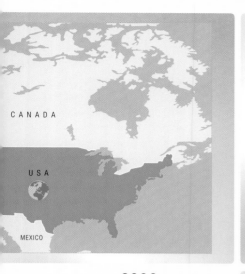

2006
INTERACTIVE TV
Digital TV households
as a proportion
of all TV households
projected 1997 percentages
borders 1998

casual users

- 20% and over
- 10% – 19%
- under 10%
- no data

high-volume users

- over 20%
- 10% – 19%
- under 10%

by 2002
ONLINE MUSIC
Value of worldwide sales
predicted 1997 US $

$47 million

$505 million

$1,640 million

1997   2000   2002

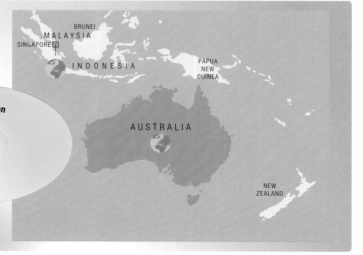

By 2003, most industrialized countries will log and analyze the movements of every citizen. Increasingly, the human body itself will be used for electronic identification: this technique, known as biometrics, includes iris scanning, DNA collection, and electronic fingerprinting. Babies could be scanned at birth, and then their electronic identity could be recognized globally.

Governments and private organizations collect vast amounts of personal information. Financial details, geographic movements and health records are stored and processed by computers that can speak easily to one another.

Modern information systems can analyze the smallest details of people's lives. Supermarkets record spending habits. Manufacturers know who is buying their goods. Marketing companies exploit these personal preferences. The 21st century computer program will be able to create comprehensive personal profiles.

Privacy can be the first casualty of surveillance. Cash machines and electronic road tolls may be useful or even necessary but they will establish a real-time geographic tracking system over entire countries. Closed circuit television (CCTV) may reduce crime in city centers but it also creates a means of enforcing public order on an unprecedented scale. Identity cards may be a weapon against criminals but they can be used as a tool of authority against the ordinary citizen.

Some form of privacy law exists in many countries. In almost all cases, it provides wholesale exemptions for police and national security agencies, and justifies surveillance by government departments, public health authorities and tax agencies on the basis of public interest.

Sources: see pages 122–5

1998
PRIVACY LAWS
in Europe, North America and Mexico

- comprehensive privacy laws
  freedom of information laws are in force; Privacy Commissioners able to act decisively on complaints

- moderate privacy laws
  Privacy Commissioners have limited powers

- weak privacy laws
  wide exemptions for law enforcement and national security

- no data

2003
EYE SPY
Government surveillance
predicted 1998
borders 1998

- total surveillance
  comprehensive, co-ordinated surveillance of lifestyle, movements, friendships, sexual and political activities, religious practices, and other data collected and processed without legal or constitutional protections

- mass surveillance
  comprehensive, co-ordinated surveillance with legal and/or constitutional protections

- high-density surveillance
  selective co-ordinated surveillance of large numbers of people using limited technological infrastructure

- medium-density surveillance
  in law enforcement, taxation, government benefits, credit reporting and financial institutions with limited legal and/or constitutional protections

- moderate surveillance
  with adequate protections

- no data

Surveillance

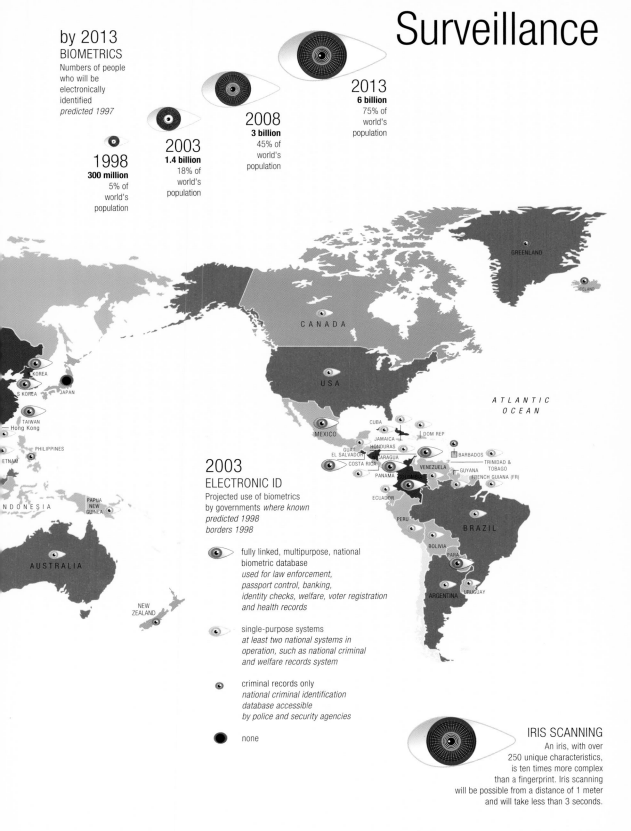

by 2013
BIOMETRICS
Numbers of people who will be electronically identified
predicted 1997

1998
300 million
5% of world's population

2003
1.4 billion
18% of world's population

2008
3 billion
45% of world's population

2013
6 billion
75% of world's population

GREENLAND

ICELAND

CANADA

USA

KOREA

S KOREA

JAPAN

TAIWAN
Hong Kong

PHILIPPINES

VETNAM

NDONESIA

PAPUA
NEW
GUINEA

AUSTRALIA

NEW
ZEALAND

ATLANTIC OCEAN

CUBA
JAMAICA
DOM REP
MEXICO
HONDURAS
GUAT
EL SALVADOR
COSTA RICA
NICARAGUA
PANAMA
BARBADOS
TRINIDAD &
TOBAGO
VENEZUELA
GUYANA
FRENCH GUIANA (FR)
COLOMBIA
ECUADOR
PERU
BRAZIL
BOLIVIA
PARA
ARGENTINA
URUGUAY

2003
ELECTRONIC ID
Projected use of biometrics by governments *where known*
predicted 1998
borders 1998

fully linked, multipurpose, national biometric database
used for law enforcement, passport control, banking, identity checks, welfare, voter registration and health records

single-purpose systems
at least two national systems in operation, such as national criminal and welfare records system

criminal records only
national criminal identification database accessible by police and security agencies

IRIS SCANNING
An iris, with over 250 unique characteristics, is ten times more complex than a fingerprint. Iris scanning will be possible from a distance of 1 meter and will take less than 3 seconds.

In many parts of the world, road building has reached saturation point, and traffic congestion is forcing new approaches to traffic management.

In the future, information technology should be able to transform our transportation systems. Zero Emission Vehicles, operated by electric batteries instead of non-renewable fuel, will reduce pollution greatly. Electronic surveillance by optical, radio, acoustic, inductive, and satellite systems will improve traffic flows.

Control centers will send information on congestion, accidents, or other hazards directly to drivers. Electronic payment systems will automate toll and fare collection.

Through the internet, drivers will be able to organize travel in advance – or en route, via third generation cellphones capable of mobile multimedia. Future cellphones will also give directions and help to make automatic emergency calls, triggered by airbag inflation.

Road vehicles will be increasingly automatic, with vision enhancement, head-up displays, collision-avoidance radar, and automatic co-operative cruise control. They will be able to travel in convoy – a "car train" – along highways fitted with guidance infrastructure, such as magnetic studs or underground cabling.

Sources: see pages 122–5

2005

AUTOMATIC DRIVER ASSISTANCE

underground cable connecting beacons carries information about weather, laws, and hazards from universal roadside processor

language-independent synthetic speech warns driver of "fog ahead"

microwave roadside beacon transmits speed limits and warnings to passing vehicles

computer

speed control

receiver

2008

"CAR TRAIN"
automatic cooperative cruise control

Traffic

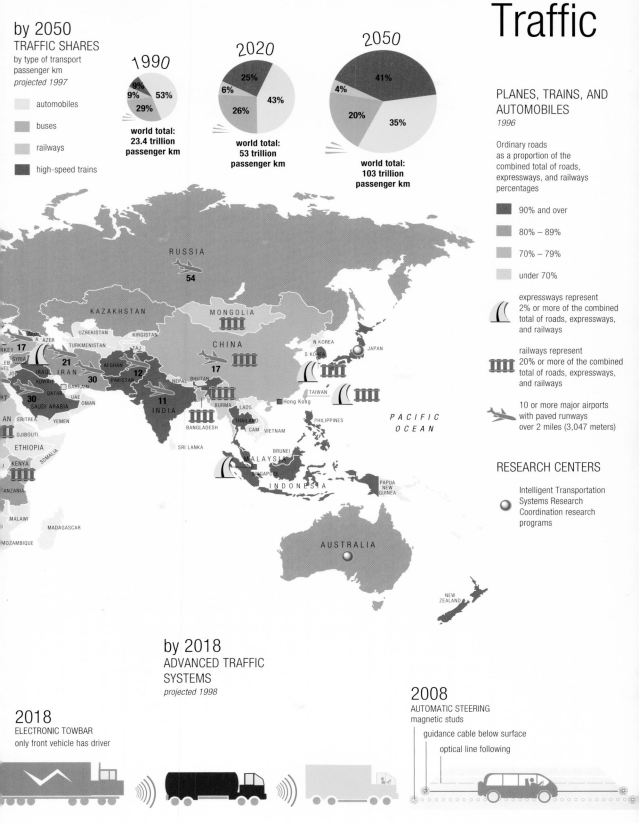

by 2050
TRAFFIC SHARES
by type of transport
passenger km
projected 1997

- automobiles
- buses
- railways
- high-speed trains

1990

9%
9%
29%
53%

**world total:
23.4 trillion
passenger km**

2020

25%
6%
26%
43%

**world total:
53 trillion
passenger km**

2050

41%
4%
20%
35%

**world total:
103 trillion
passenger km**

PLANES, TRAINS, AND AUTOMOBILES
1996

Ordinary roads
as a proportion of the
combined total of roads,
expressways, and railways
percentages

- 90% and over
- 80% − 89%
- 70% − 79%
- under 70%

expressways represent
2% or more of the combined
total of roads, expressways,
and railways

railways represent
20% or more of the combined
total of roads, expressways,
and railways

10 or more major airports
with paved runways
over 2 miles (3,047 meters)

RESEARCH CENTERS

Intelligent Transportation
Systems Research
Coordination research
programs

Map labels

RUSSIA 54

KAZAKHSTAN

MONGOLIA

CHINA 17

N KOREA
S KOREA
JAPAN

UZBEKISTAN
KIRGISTAN
TURKMENISTAN
TAJ

AZER
SYRIA 17
IRAQ
IRAN 21
KUWAIT
QATAR
BAHRAIN
UAE
OMAN
SAUDI ARABIA 30

AFGHAN
PAKISTAN 30
12

NEPAL BHUTAN
INDIA 11
BURMA
BANGLADESH
LAOS
THAILAND
CAM
VIETNAM

TAIWAN
Hong Kong

YEMEN
ERITREA
DJIBOUTI
ETHIOPIA
KENYA
SOMALIA
TANZANIA
MALAWI
MADAGASCAR
MOZAMBIQUE

SRI LANKA

PHILIPPINES

PACIFIC OCEAN

BRUNEI
MALAYSIA
SINGAPORE
INDONESIA

PAPUA NEW GUINEA

AUSTRALIA

NEW ZEALAND

by 2018
ADVANCED TRAFFIC SYSTEMS
projected 1998

2018
ELECTRONIC TOWBAR
only front vehicle has driver

2008
AUTOMATIC STEERING
magnetic studs
guidance cable below surface
optical line following

The Future of
Globalization

By 2020, world population growth, economic growth, and developments in technology will have doubled the number of international travelers for business and pleasure, compared with 1995. Increased leisure time and the globalization of business will also play their part.

To improve capacity and cut down delays, there will be ticketless travel, automatic security checks, larger planes and integrated transport systems.

More people will arrange their own personalized travel and holidays via the internet and digital television.

Tourism is the world's largest industry and its economic impact will grow in rich and poor countries alike. In 1997, travel and tourism represented nearly a third of the economy of the Caribbean and 12 percent of the economy of the European Union.

By 2007, many rich countries will see a big increase in jobs in travel and tourism. But as the tourist industry grows, most of the new jobs will be in Asia. In North East Asia including China, the number of tourism jobs could rise by as many as 64 million. The fastest rate of growth may be in South East Asia, where an additional 21 million jobs could be created.

In 1997, France was the world's most popular destination. By 2007, it will have been surpassed by both China and the USA.

The first bookings for space holidays have already been taken.

Sources: see pages 122–5

The Atlas of the Future Copyright © Myriad Editions Limited

by 2017
AIR TRAFFIC

Huge planes, or superjumbos, seating up to 1,000 in the wings, are being developed to carry the increasing number of air travelers, rising from 1.6 billion in 1997 to nearly 5 billion by 2017.

248 m

2.4 million

897,000

322,000

496,000

529,000

2007
JOBS IN TOURISM

Percentage increase in OECD countries
2007 compared with 1997 projected 1997

■ increase of 30% or more

■ 20% – 29% increase

■ 10% – 19% increase

□ under 10% increase

□ other countries

▽ over 300,000 new jobs projected

Tourism

1995
564 million international arrivals

2020
1,602 million international arrivals

EUROPE including former USSR
771 m

MIDDLE EAST
SOUTH ASIA
EAST ASIA / PACIFIC

AFRICA
69 m

35 m

17 m

462 m

by 2020
INTERNATIONAL TOURIST ARRIVALS
by region
projected 1997

- over 500 million
- 300 – 500 million
- 100 – 300 million
- under 100 million

INTERNATIONAL TOURIST DEPARTURES
by region
projected 1997 millions

- over 500 million
- 300 - 500 million
- 100 - 300 million
- under 100 million

2020
WORLD'S TOP DESTINATIONS
Number of tourists
projected 1998
millions

1 China 137 m
2 USA 102 m
3 France 93 m
4 Spain 71 m
5 Hong Kong 59 m
6 Italy 53 m
7 UK 53 m
8 Mexico 49 m
9 Russia 47 m
10 Czech Republic 44 m

New technology and the global superhighway may have an even greater impact on work than the industrial revolution.

With the growth of manufacturing, workers moved away from agriculture. At the end of the 20th century, workers no longer needed in manufacturing are being absorbed by services and a growing information economy.

As new technology increases productivity, it may be possible for all goods and services to be provided by a small proportion of the potential working population.

Most information services can be provided from anywhere in the world. More countries will become specialist outsourcing centers for jobs in information. The globalizing labor market means that more companies will move jobs to places offering skilled but cheap labor.

More people will work part time, be self-employed or move into the informal economy. More will go abroad or even across the world in search of work. By 2010, more than 40 percent of the paid workforce will be women.

There will be greater inequality between those with jobs and those without, and between the information-rich and information-poor. The prosperous will employ more people for personal services – for health care and education as well as cleaning and child care.

Sources: see pages 122–5

NORTH AMERICA

29 million

94 million

LATIN AMERICA AND THE CARIBBEAN

INDUSTRIAL ROBOTS
at work in Japan
numbers

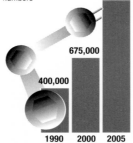

		1.2m
	675,000	
400,000		
1990	2000	2005

Work

by 2010
MORE WORKERS
Change in share
of population in paid work
percentage points
*2010 compared with 1990
projected 1997*

growth

- over 9 percentage
  points increase
- 6.1 - 9
- 3.1 - 6
- up to 3

decline

- up to 3
- 3.1 and over

OUTSOURCING

 centers for outsourcing work
as a result of new technology

by 2010
MORE WOMEN AT WORK
Increase of women's
share of the paid workforce
by region, percentage points
*2010 compared with 1990
projected 1997*

- over 4 percentage
  points increase
- 2 - 4
- up to 2
- little or no change

WORKFORCE BY REGION
Increase in total workforce
2010 compared with 1990

10 million additional workers
figures rounded

Note: Based on
UN population data 1996

10 million

4 million

204 million

599 million

4 million

71

The globalization of business looks set to continue. Despite economic tremors in Asia in the late 1990s, countries will continue to open up their markets to foreign capital and to invest abroad.

The Atlas of the Future Copyright © Myriad Editions Limited

The world economy is becoming a single market for labor, production facilities, and finance. From 1992 to 1997, the number of transnational corporations grew by 27 percent, while the number of foreign affiliates grew by 88 percent. This trend is likely to accelerate. A significant proportion of growth is coming from developing countries.

From 1993 to 1995, the foreign assets of the top 100 transnationals, worth 1.7 trillion US dollars, grew at 30 percent per year. In 1995, more than half the top 300 transnationals expected a marked increase in the sums they would invest abroad by 2001.

Fueling these trends is the increasing internationalization of currency and equity markets.

Sources:
see pages 122–5

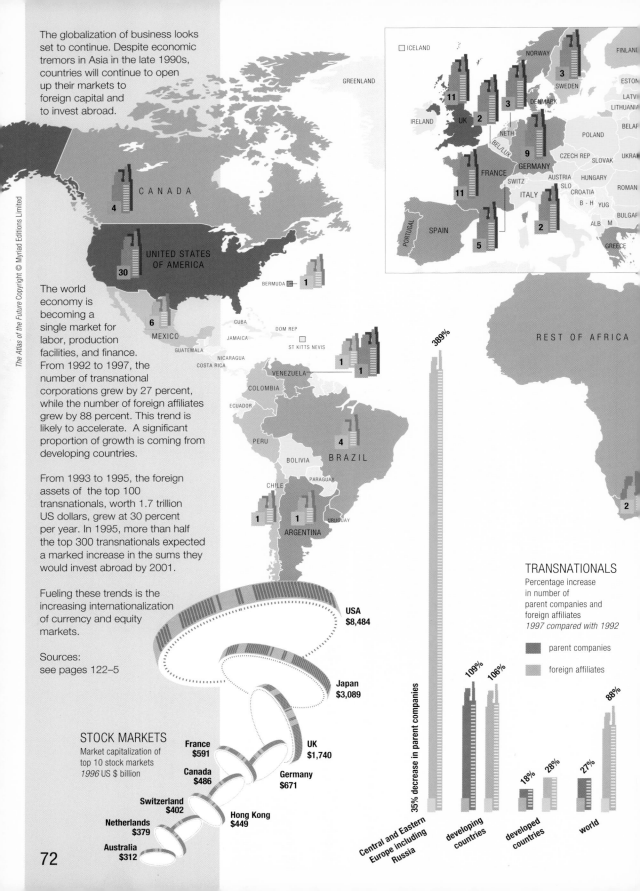

ICELAND

GREENLAND

NORWAY
SWEDEN 3
11 UK 2 3 DENMARK
IRELAND
NETH
BELILUX
9 GERMANY
7 FRANCE
11 SWITZ AUSTRIA HUNGARY
ITALY SLO CROATIA
5 2 B - H YUG
PORTUGAL SPAIN ALB
GREECE
FINLAN
ESTON
LATVI
LITHUANIA
BELAF
POLAND
CZECH REP SLOVAK
UKRA
ROMAN
BULGAF
M

CANADA 4

UNITED STATES OF AMERICA 30

BERMUDA 1

MEXICO 6

CUBA
JAMAICA
DOM REP
ST KITTS NEVIS
GUATEMALA
NICARAGUA
COSTA RICA
VENEZUELA 1 1

COLOMBIA
ECUADOR
PERU
BRAZIL 4
BOLIVIA
PARAGUAY
CHILE 1
ARGENTINA 1
URUGUAY

REST OF AFRICA

2

STOCK MARKETS
Market capitalization of top 10 stock markets
1996 US $ billion

USA $8,484

Japan $3,089

UK $1,740

France $591
Canada $486
Germany $671
Switzerland $402
Hong Kong $449
Netherlands $379
Australia $312

TRANSNATIONALS
Percentage increase in number of parent companies and foreign affiliates
1997 compared with 1992

- parent companies
- foreign affiliates

389%

35% decrease in parent companies

Central and Eastern Europe including Russia

109% 106%
developing countries

18% 28%
developed countries

27% 88%
world

72

Business

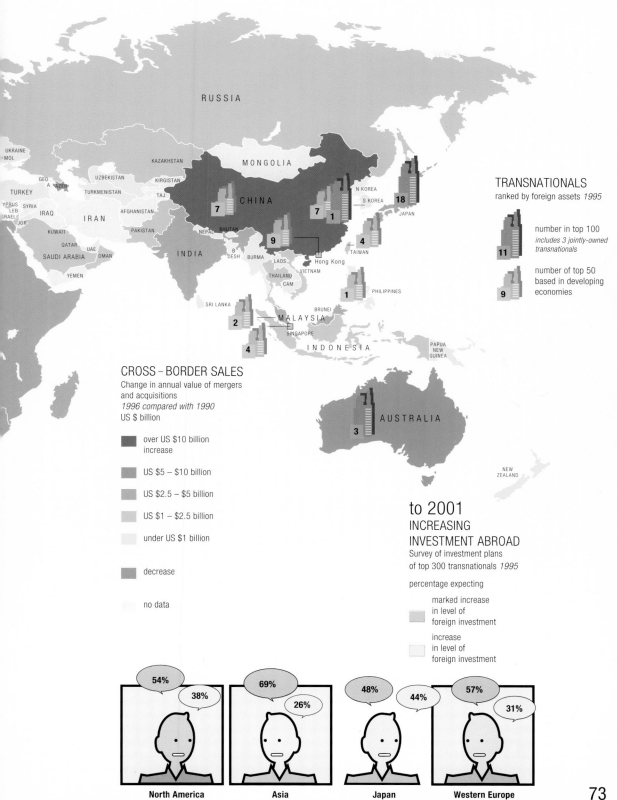

RUSSIA

MONGOLIA

CHINA   **7**   **7** **1**

9

N KOREA
S KOREA
18   JAPAN

4   TAIWAN

Hong Kong

1   PHILIPPINES

SRI LANKA

2   MALAYSIA

BRUNEI

SINGAPORE

4   INDONESIA

PAPUA
NEW
GUINEA

UKRAINE
-MOL
KAZAKHSTAN
KIRGISTAN
UZBEKISTAN
TURKMENISTAN
TAJ
GEO
A AZER
TURKEY
CYPRUS SYRIA
LEB
ISRAEL
JOR
IRAQ
IRAN
AFGHANISTAN
PAKISTAN
KUWAIT
QATAR
UAE
OMAN
SAUDI ARABIA
YEMEN
INDIA
NEPAL BHUTAN
B
DESH   BURMA
LAOS
THAILAND
CAM
VIETNAM

AUSTRALIA

3

NEW
ZEALAND

TRANSNATIONALS
ranked by foreign assets *1995*

11   number in top 100
*includes 3 jointly-owned
transnationals*

9   number of top 50
based in developing
economies

CROSS – BORDER SALES
Change in annual value of mergers
and acquisitions
1996 compared with 1990
US $ billion

- over US $10 billion increase
- US $5 – $10 billion
- US $2.5 – $5 billion
- US $1 – $2.5 billion
- under US $1 billion
- decrease
- no data

to 2001
INCREASING
INVESTMENT ABROAD
Survey of investment plans
of top 300 transnationals *1995*

percentage expecting

- marked increase
in level of
foreign investment
- increase
in level of
foreign investment

54% / 38%	69% / 26%	48% / 44%	57% / 31%
North America	**Asia**	**Japan**	**Western Europe**

73

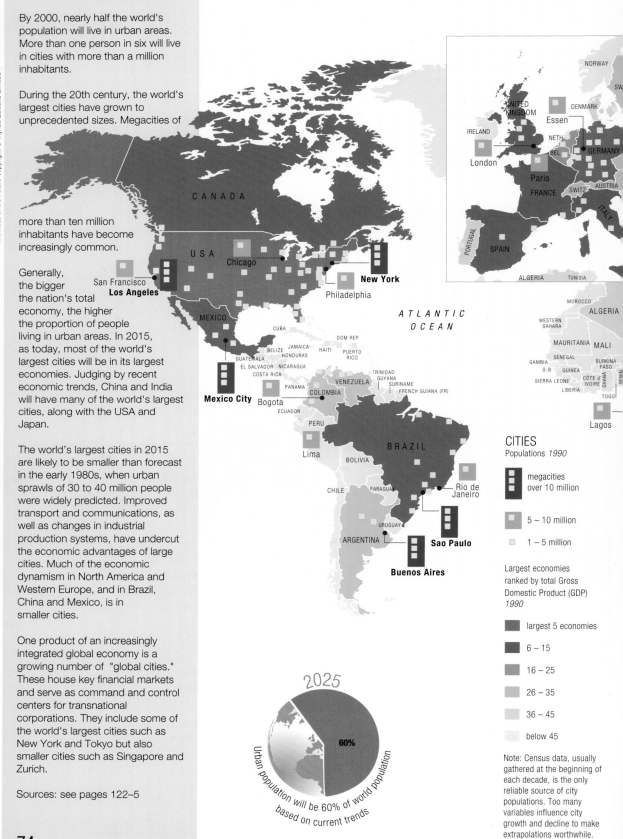

By 2000, nearly half the world's population will live in urban areas. More than one person in six will live in cities with more than a million inhabitants.

During the 20th century, the world's largest cities have grown to unprecedented sizes. Megacities of more than ten million inhabitants have become increasingly common.

Generally, the bigger the nation's total economy, the higher the proportion of people living in urban areas. In 2015, as today, most of the world's largest cities will be in its largest economies. Judging by recent economic trends, China and India will have many of the world's largest cities, along with the USA and Japan.

The world's largest cities in 2015 are likely to be smaller than forecast in the early 1980s, when urban sprawls of 30 to 40 million people were widely predicted. Improved transport and communications, as well as changes in industrial production systems, have undercut the economic advantages of large cities. Much of the economic dynamism in North America and Western Europe, and in Brazil, China and Mexico, is in smaller cities.

One product of an increasingly integrated global economy is a growing number of "global cities." These house key financial markets and serve as command and control centers for transnational corporations. They include some of the world's largest cities such as New York and Tokyo but also smaller cities such as Singapore and Zurich.

Sources: see pages 122–5

ATLANTIC OCEAN

CANADA

USA

Chicago

San Francisco
Los Angeles

New York
Philadelphia

MEXICO

CUBA
DOM REP
JAMAICA HAITI PUERTO RICO
BELIZE HONDURAS
GUATEMALA
EL SALVADOR NICARAGUA
COSTA RICA
PANAMA
VENEZUELA
TRINIDAD
GUYANA
SURINAME
FRENCH GUIANA (FR)

Mexico City Bogota
COLOMBIA
ECUADOR
PERU
Lima
BOLIVIA
BRAZIL
Rio de Janeiro
CHILE
PARAGUAY
URUGUAY
ARGENTINA
Sao Paulo
Buenos Aires

NORWAY
SW
UNITED KINGDOM
DENMARK
Essen
IRELAND
NETH
GERMANY
London
BEL
Paris
FRANCE
SWITZ
AUSTRIA
ITALY
PORTUGAL
SPAIN
ALGERIA TUNISIA

MOROCCO
ALGERIA
WESTERN SAHARA
MAURITANIA MALI
GAMBIA SENEGAL BURKINA FASO
G-B GUINEA
SIERRA LEONE CÔTE d'IVOIRE GHANA BENIN
LIBERIA TOGO
Lagos

CITIES
Populations *1990*

megacities over 10 million

5 – 10 million

1 – 5 million

Largest economies ranked by total Gross Domestic Product (GDP) *1990*

largest 5 economies

6 – 15

16 – 25

26 – 35

36 – 45

below 45

Note: Census data, usually gathered at the beginning of each decade, is the only reliable source of city populations. Too many variables influence city growth and decline to make extrapolations worthwhile.

2025

60%

Urban population will be 60% of world population based on current trends

74

Cities

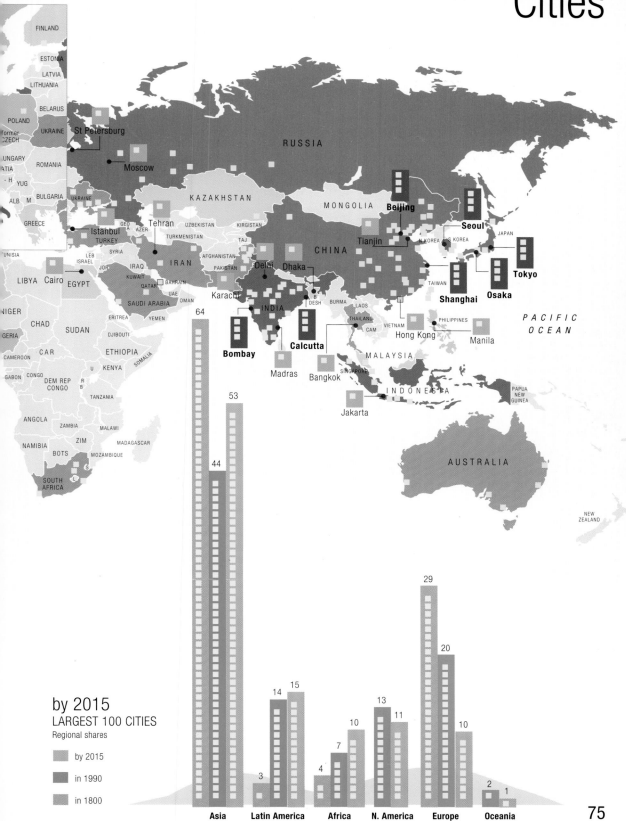

FINLAND
ESTONIA
LATVIA
LITHUANIA
BELARUS
POLAND
former
CZECH
UNGARY
ATIA
– H
YUG
ALB M BULGARIA
GREECE
ROMANIA
UKRAINE

St Petersburg
Moscow

RUSSIA

KAZAKHSTAN

MONGOLIA

Beijing

Seoul
JAPAN
Tianjin
N KOREA S KOREA

UZBEKISTAN
KIRGISTAN
TURKMENISTAN
TAJ
AFGHANISTAN
PAKISTAN

Tehran
IRAN
Istanbul
TURKEY
AZER
GEO
A
SYRIA
LEB
ISRAEL
JOR
IRAQ
KUWAIT
QATAR
BAHRAIN
UAE
OMAN
SAUDI ARABIA
YEMEN

TUNISIA
LIBYA Cairo
EGYPT
NIGER
CHAD
SUDAN
ERITREA
DJIBOUTI
GERIA
CAMEROON
CAR
ETHIOPIA
KENYA
SOMALIA
GABON CONGO
DEM REP
CONGO
R
B
TANZANIA
ANGOLA ZAMBIA MALAWI
NAMIBIA
ZIM
MADAGASCAR
BOTS
MOZAMBIQUE
S
SOUTH
AFRICA

Delhi   Dhaka
CHINA
Karachi
INDIA
B
DESH
BURMA
LAOS
THAILAND
CAM
VIETNAM
Shanghai
Osaka
Tokyo

TAIWAN

Hong Kong

PHILIPPINES
Manila

PACIFIC
OCEAN

64

Bombay

Calcutta
53

Madras
Bangkok
MALAYSIA
SINGAPORE

44

Jakarta
INDONESIA

PAPUA
NEW
GUINEA

AUSTRALIA

NEW
ZEALAND

by 2015
LARGEST 100 CITIES
Regional shares

by 2015
in 1990
in 1800

Asia
64
53
44

Latin America
14 15
3

Africa
4 7 10

N. America
13 11

Europe
29
20
10

Oceania
2 1

75

The market economy will continue to gain ground worldwide. During the 1990s a further 28 countries began to establish market-based systems, though the transition will go on well into the new century.

Globalization means that the wellbeing of other states' economies will become ever more central to all.

This interdependence was confirmed in 1997–98 by the impact of financial tremors in Asia on Western economies.

Despite widespread criticism of their demands for stringent market reforms, the International Monetary Fund (IMF) and World Bank will continue to be the main international providers of rescue packages and loans for states in difficulty.

The future of the Group of Seven is an open question. A few states with strong or rapidly growing economies will strive to exert greater political and economic influence in the new century.

The North American Free Trade Association (NAFTA) may eventually become a huge trading bloc, the Free Trade Area of the Americas. There has also been an explosion of smaller free trade agreements intended to boost regional trade.

Sources: see pages 122–5

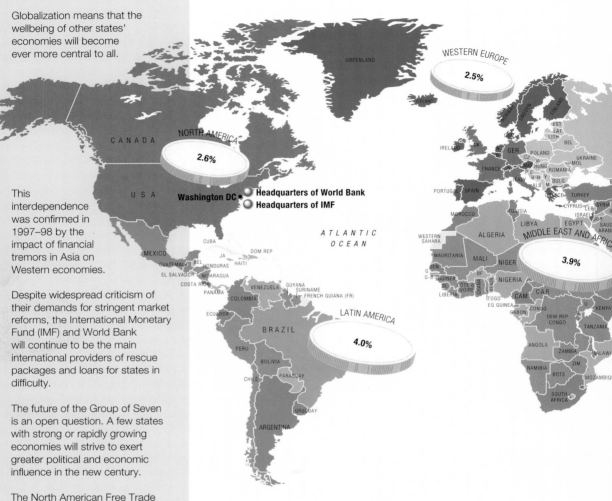

WESTERN EUROPE
2.5%

NORTH AMERICA
2.6%

Washington DC ● ○ **Headquarters of World Bank**
○ **Headquarters of IMF**

ATLANTIC OCEAN

MIDDLE EAST AND AFRICA
3.9%

LATIN AMERICA
4.0%

by 2002
ECONOMIC MONETARY UNION (EMU)

member states of the European Union likely to join the first round of EMU *1999–2002*

other EU member states

other states

Economies

2001-2006
World trade: average annual growth 7.1%

EASTERN EUROPE
4.1%

RUSSIA

KAZAKHSTAN

MONGOLIA

UZBEK   KIRGIS
TURKMEN
TAJ

N KOREA
S KOREA

JAPAN

IRAN   AFGHAN   CHINA

ASIA AND AUSTRALASIA

KUWAIT
BAHRAIN   PAKISTAN   NEPAL BHUTAN
AR UAE   OMAN
EMEN

INDIA   DESH BURMA   LAOS
THAI
CAM   VIETNAM

TAIWAN

Hong Kong

6.4%

SOMALIA

SRI LANKA

PHILIPPINES

MALAYSIA
SINGAPORE

INDONESIA

PAPUA
NEW
GUINEA

DAGASCAR

AUSTRALIA

NEW
ZEALAND

THE IMF CLASSIFICATION OF ECONOMIES
1997

advanced economies:

- Group of Seven (G7)
- other advanced economies
- transitional economies

developing economies
by main sources of export income:

- manufacturing
- fuel
- primary goods:
  food and raw materials
- services, money sent home
- diverse sources
- no data

1997-2001
ECONOMIC GROWTH

Average annual growth of
gross domestic product (GDP)
by region *projected early 1997*

THE 10 BIG EMERGING MARKETS
early 21st century
*as predicted by
US Department of Commerce, 1997*

POLAND

TURKEY   CHINA   SOUTH KOREA

INDIA

MEXICO

INDONESIA

BRAZIL

SOUTH AFRICA

ARGENTINA

Until 2005 at least, India and Japan, as well as states in Western Europe, North America, and Australasia, are likely to remain liberal democracies.

Much of the Middle East and North Africa, in addition to China, will probably remain authoritarian.

The rest of the world may be less stable politically. Sub-Saharan Africa will probably be the least stable region, and its fragile new liberal democracies may well revert to authoritarian regimes.

In Latin America, democratic values are still vulnerable to challenges from the military and other elites.

China shapes political trends in East and South East Asia, and as long as it remains authoritarian, any democratization in the region is likely to be halting and cautious.

Sources: see pages 122–5

GREENLAND

ICELAND

NORWAY
SWEDEN
FINLAND
ESTONIA
LATVIA
LITHUANIA
BELARUS
DENMARK
IRELAND
UNITED KINGDOM
NETH
BEL
GERMANY
POLAND
UKRAINE
CZECH REP
SLOVAK
FRANCE
SWITZ
AUSTRIA
HUNGARY
SLO
ROMANIA
CROATIA
ITALY
B-H
YUG
BULGARIA
PORTUGAL
SPAIN
ALB
M
GREECE

CANADA

UNITED STATES OF AMERICA

ATLANTIC OCEAN

MEXICO
CUBA
DOM REP
BEL
HONDURAS
JA
HAITI
GUATEMALA
EL SALVADOR
NICARAGUA
COSTA RICA
PANAMA
VENEZUELA
TRINIDAD & TOBAGO
SURINAME
GUYANA
FRENCH GUIANA (FR)
COLOMBIA
ECUADOR
PERU
BRAZIL
BOLIVIA
PARAGUAY
CHILE
ARGENTINA
URUGUAY

TUNISIA
MOROCCO
ALGERIA
LIBYA
WESTERN SAHARA
MAURITANIA
MALI
NIGER
CHAD
CAPE VERDE
SENEGAL
GAMBIA
GUINEA-BISSAU
GUINEA
SIERRA LEONE
CÔTE d'IVOIRE
GHANA
BENIN
NIGERIA
CAR
LIBERIA
TOGO
CAMEROON
EQ GUINEA
GABON
CONGO
ZAIRE
ANGOLA
ZAM
NAMIBIA
BOT
SOUTH AFRICA

2005
FUTURE REGIMES

States

likely to remain liberal democratic

likely to remain authoritarian

likely to be unstable
moving toward either liberal democracy or authoritarianism, or toward a regime combining democratic and authoritarian features

Democracy

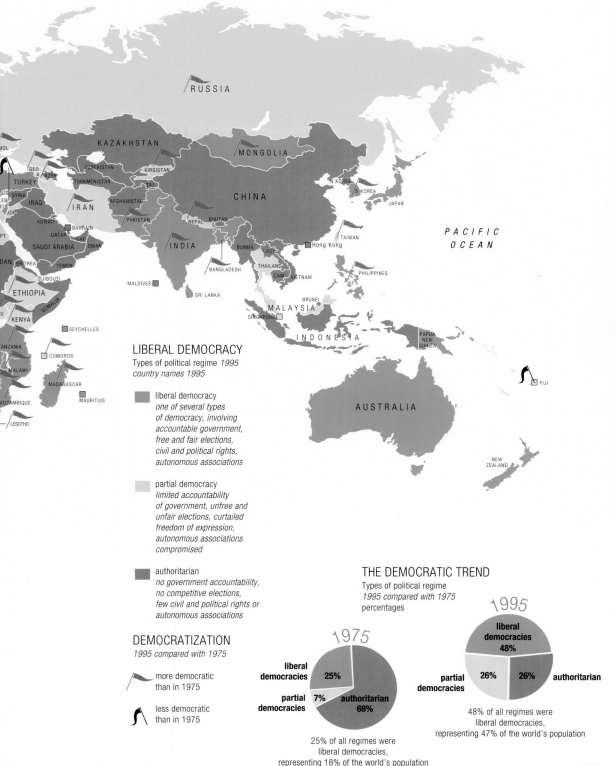

LIBERAL DEMOCRACY

Types of political regime *1995*
country names *1995*

liberal democracy
*one of several types
of democracy, involving
accountable government,
free and fair elections,
civil and political rights,
autonomous associations*

partial democracy
*limited accountability
of government, unfree and
unfair elections, curtailed
freedom of expression,
autonomous associations
compromised*

authoritarian
*no government accountability,
no competitive elections,
few civil and political rights or
autonomous associations*

DEMOCRATIZATION

1995 compared with 1975

more democratic
than in 1975

less democratic
than in 1975

THE DEMOCRATIC TREND

Types of political regime
1995 compared with 1975
percentages

1975

liberal
democracies **25%**

partial
democracies **7%**

authoritarian
68%

25% of all regimes were
liberal democracies,
representing 18% of the world's population

1995

liberal
democracies
48%

partial
democracies **26%**

26% authoritarian

48% of all regimes were
liberal democracies,
representing 47% of the world's population

Millitary science and technology are revolutionizing warfare. Developments in surveillance will enable enemy forces to be located, identified and continuously tracked in real time. Developments in target acquisition, guidance systems and warhead design will ensure that targets – tanks, aircraft, warships or humans – are damaged beyond repair.

The destructive power of new munitions and the precision of their delivery may mean that future battlefields become too lethal for humans to fight on. Warfare between industrialized countries will become increasingly automated. Robots, robot-driven armored vehicles, pilotless aircraft and computerized missiles will advance on enemy territory with little direct human intervention. Technology may improve military capabilities to the extent that war between industrialized countries is unknown.

The gulf in military capability between the rich world and the poor world will continue to grow throughout the 21st century. There will be countries rich enough to fight high-technology wars and those which can only afford very basic arsenals.

Most wars will be civil wars. Most interstate wars will be between developing countries using soldiers and conventional weapons. War between a high-tech and a low-tech military power could end rapidly in the annihilation of the latter.

By 2050, weapons of mass destruction – biological, chemical and nuclear – delivered by long-range ballistic missiles, will be within the capacity of many states and within the grasp of terrorist groups.

Another terrorist threat will be the attack on a nation's computer systems causing the total shutdown of its economy. High technology alone will not guarantee protection from terrorism or from military rivals.

Sources: see pages 122–5

The Atlas of the Future Copyright © Myriad Editions Limited

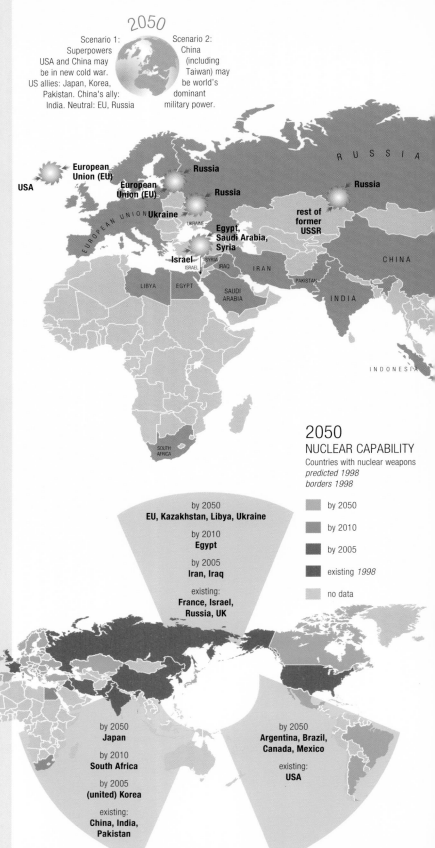

2050

Scenario 1: Superpowers USA and China may be in new cold war. US allies: Japan, Korea, Pakistan. China's ally: India. Neutral: EU, Russia

Scenario 2: China (including Taiwan) may be world's dominant military power.

2050
NUCLEAR CAPABILITY

Countries with nuclear weapons
predicted 1998
borders 1998

- by 2050
- by 2010
- by 2005
- existing *1998*
- no data

by 2050
EU, Kazakhstan, Libya, Ukraine

by 2010
Egypt

by 2005
Iran, Iraq

existing:
France, Israel, Russia, UK

by 2050
Japan

by 2010
South Africa

by 2005
(united) Korea

existing:
China, India, Pakistan

by 2050
Argentina, Brazil, Canada, Mexico

existing:
USA

Military Might

2050
DEADLY WEAPONS
predicted 1998
borders 2050

- countries able to deliver biological, chemical and/or nuclear weapons by ballistic missile *mid 21st century*
- other countries

REGIONAL RIVALRY

- regional military rivals *mid 21st century*

Japan, (united) Korea
KOREA   JAPAN

PACIFIC OCEAN

Indonesia

Australia

AUSTRALIA

CANADA

USA

European Union (EU)

BRAZIL

Argentina   Brazil

ARGENTINA

TERRORISM
Terrorist weapons of the future

- electronic shutdown of enemy's economy
- enemy's TV broadcasts heavily manipulated
- enemy's air traffic control computers scrambled

2050
EVOLUTION OF THE US SOLDIER

SOLDIER
Unable to operate sophisticated weaponry
|
High casualty risk: emotionally and physically fallible
|
Expensive to train

CYBER SOLDIER
Psychotropic drugs block stress, fear, nausea, heat and cold, and fatigue
|
Smart fabric suit maintains body temperature. If bullet pierces cloth, powdered antiseptic is released to treat wound immediately
|
Sensors monitor blood and pulse. Microphone monitors heart and breathing

Maps and rifle-sight information go directly to retina without obscuring vision
|
Accurate navigation day and night to within one meter

Video camera sends pictures back to base
|
Laser rifle sight allows accurate firing or firing from base by remote control
|
Binoculars use satellite to pinpoint objects

ROBOT SOLDIERS
100% subordinate, 24 hour working day, no training cost, low production cost
|
Impervious to physical or emotional weakness, extreme temperatures, frost and fire, and biological, chemical and nuclear weapons

Insect-like robots perform wide range of tasks, including surveillance, mine laying and detection, firing weapons

By 2050, the United Nations will be less confined to peacekeeping and more concerned with peace making and peace enforcement.

One view is that the UN would concentrate on global policing. It would no longer be dependent on military units temporarily assigned from a few member states, able only to monitor ceasefires, but would use its own permanent forces to enforce peace.

A scenario based on local solutions seems more likely. In this, the UN would become an umbrella organization for a range of autonomous regional security groupings, such as the European Union, the Organization of Central American States, the Organization of African Unity, and the Arab League. These would provide their own financial and military resources for peace making and peace enforcement. The UN would still provide assistance, such as intelligence data gathered by its network of surveillance satellites, but would not be responsible for resources and personnel on the ground.

The UN has established a large number of international specialized agencies to deal with such issues as world health, refugees, food distribution, environmental protection and children's welfare. The success of these, marked by a new era of cooperation between world governments, may signal the way ahead for the UN Security Council. By 2050, the UN may be able to fulfill its orginal task of establishing a permanent international system to oversee global peace and security.

Sources: see pages 122–5

The Atlas of the Future Copyright © Myriad Editions Limited

2010

EU replaces France and UK to join China, Russia, and USA as permanent members of Security Council.

Brazil, India, Japan, and South Africa also become new permanent members.

United Nations

2050
MILITARY REGIONAL ALLIANCES
predicted 1998
borders 2050

- European Union
- in association with European Union
- Association of Central Asian Muslim states
- Organization of Central American States
- Organization of South American States
- North America
- Arab League
- Organization of African Unity
- Association of South Asian Nations
- Japan/Korea Alliance
- China

PEACEKEEPING

- countries supplying troops for UN peacekeeping operations *1996*
- UN peacekeeping operations *1997*
- use of military forces to control terrorism *1990s*

NATURAL DISASTERS

- militaries that responded to natural disasters *1996-97*

83

Into the
Unknown

Nanotechnology deals in dimensions of less than a ten thousandth of a millimeter, and in machines measured in molecules rather than in metal parts.

Nanotechnology is an embryonic science. Its goal is to manipulate matter at the atomic level. In the early 1990s, researchers at IBM were the first to write logos and messages in individual atoms. This pointed the way to the promise of atomically accurate machines: built atom by atom to create a flawless, perfectly sound structure. Such a machine has yet to be made but many predict that nanotechnology will be part of our everyday life in the 21st century (see **High-Tech Health**, pages 32–3).

The earliest applications of nanotechnology are likely to be in computing and engineering. By 2015, nanochips may provide faster and cheaper computing and communications.

One of the most revolutionary aspects of nanotechnology could be self-assembly. If the robots, or nanites, that populate a nanofactory could make copies of and repair themselves, and adapt to different environments, they would mimic biological cells in their complexity. If self-assembly proves to be a practical concept, nanotechnology could transform materials and manufacturing. In theory, anything from a chair to an aircraft could be built by billions of self-assembling nanodevices. For example, we could make milk from a mixture of grass, air and water by rearranging the atoms, or build furniture that rearranges itself to fit our particular needs or shapes.

There may be a downside to nanotechnology. Nanodevices could be used to proliferate the production of superweapons. At worst, we might have to deal with hostile devices that replicate themselves uncontrollably.

Sources: see pages 122–5

SELF-ASSEMBLY

One of the most revolutionary aims of nanotechnology is to design materials with a built-in set of instructions that will enable them to behave like living organisms, reproducing and repairing themselves. In this process of "self-assembly," atoms and molecules are arranged by nanorobots into ordered functioning entities without human intervention.

Nature abounds with examples of self-assembly: the properties of organisms as simple as a raindrop or as complex as a human cell are implicitly coded in their components.

MAIN CENTERS OF NANOTECHNOLOGY RESEARCH
late 1990s

USA   UK   Japan

Nanotechnology

Nanotechnology may
supplement or even
replace biotechnology
in areas of health care
such as diagnostics,
pharmaceutical delivery,
and gene therapy.

The first major impact of
nanotechnology will be on
computing. If electronics
can harness components
the size of molecules,
the potential speed of
computers would be
much greater than it is
in the late 1990s.

This may not be far away.
Feature sizes on computer
chips are already as
small as 0.25 microns,
only two and a half times
larger than 0.1 micron,
the size at which
nanotechnology
begins.

THE SCALE OF
THINGS TO COME
logarithmic scale

A nanometer is one
billionth of a meter,
one thousand times
smaller than a micron,
which is the size of
elements in
contemporary
micro electronics.

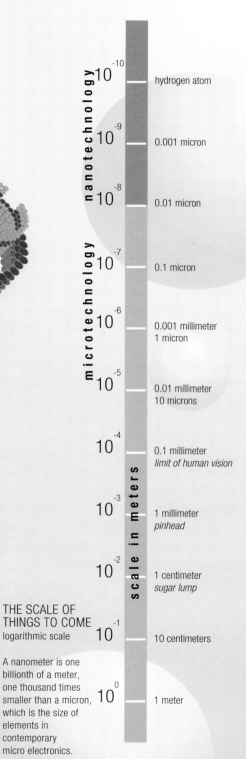

nanotechnology

10^{-10} — hydrogen atom

10^{-9} — 0.001 micron

10^{-8} — 0.01 micron

microtechnology

10^{-7} — 0.1 micron

10^{-6} — 0.001 millimeter
1 micron

10^{-5} — 0.01 millimeter
10 microns

10^{-4} — 0.1 millimeter
limit of human vision

scale in meters

10^{-3} — 1 millimeter
pinhead

10^{-2} — 1 centimeter
sugar lump

10^{-1} — 10 centimeters

10^{0} — 1 meter

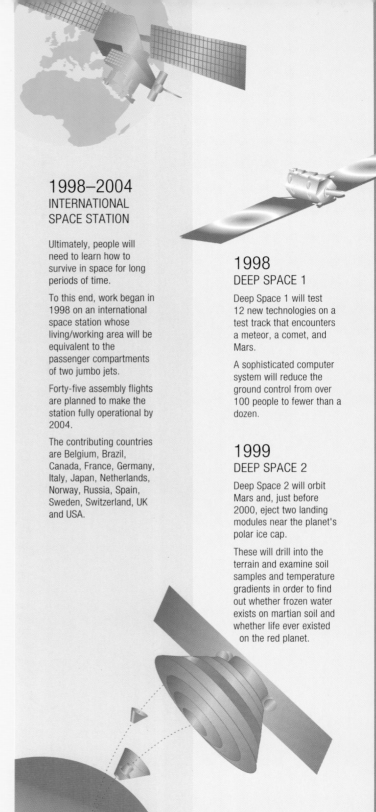

Space exploration holds the key to the origin of the universe, the fundamental workings of nature, and ultimately the survival of our species.

At the core of the near future phase of space exploration, NASA's New Millennium program will test revolutionary technologies in preparation for planned missions to explore other solar systems and search for earth-like planets.

Ground-based control of space probes is expensive and will become increasingly impractical as the probes move farther out into deep space. Deep Space 1 will be equipped with Remote Agent, a computing system that will control the craft's speed and direction as well as its self-diagnostics, fault protection and recovery systems. Also under development is an electric propulsion system that will replace today's chemical systems and should increase both the efficiency and range of future probes and landers.

Artificial intelligence is crucial to the development of space exploration (see **Artificial Intelligence**, pages 36–7). Wherever human landings are planned, robotic probes will lead the way. The rapid development in artificial intelligence aboard these probes should lead to autonomous control systems and pave the way for our first landing on Mars.

Sources: see pages 122–5

1998–2004
INTERNATIONAL SPACE STATION

Ultimately, people will need to learn how to survive in space for long periods of time.

To this end, work began in 1998 on an international space station whose living/working area will be equivalent to the passenger compartments of two jumbo jets.

Forty-five assembly flights are planned to make the station fully operational by 2004.

The contributing countries are Belgium, Brazil, Canada, France, Germany, Italy, Japan, Netherlands, Norway, Russia, Spain, Sweden, Switzerland, UK and USA.

1998
DEEP SPACE 1

Deep Space 1 will test 12 new technologies on a test track that encounters a meteor, a comet, and Mars.

A sophisticated computer system will reduce the ground control from over 100 people to fewer than a dozen.

1999
DEEP SPACE 2

Deep Space 2 will orbit Mars and, just before 2000, eject two landing modules near the planet's polar ice cap.

These will drill into the terrain and examine soil samples and temperature gradients in order to find out whether frozen water exists on martian soil and whether life ever existed on the red planet.

MARS

Space Exploration

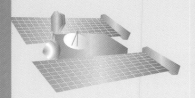

SATURN

1999
STARDUST

The earth was formed out of cosmic gas, dust and water. Stardust's mission is to collect inter-stellar dust from space to help us understand the origins of our solar system.

It will then fly through the wake of the comet Wild 2, sampling its materials. It is due to return to earth in 2006.

2001
GENESIS

The sun's particle emission will tell us more about the composition and formation of stars and planets. It will also help us to understand the astronauts' health risks from exposure to radiation. Genesis will return with its cargo of solar particles in 2003.

2002
EUROPA ORBITER

Scientists believe that water may exist under the ice on the surface of one of Jupiter's moons, Europa, and that this may support organic life. This probe will test the theory by mapping the surface of Europa and determining the thickness of its surface ice.

2004
CASSINI

Saturn's giant moon, Titan, may have atmospheric conditions similar to those when earth was first formed.

Cassini was launched in 1994 to eject the European Space Agency's Huygens lander into Titan's atmosphere.

2007
NEXT GENERATION SPACE TELESCOPE (NGST)

Around 2007, the NGST will be launched. It will fly much farther from earth than Hubble – possibly three times the distance from the earth to the Sun – and will be at least four times more powerful.

NGST will be able to detect the presence of planetary systems from their infrared emissions and will be a primary source of information for planning future explorer missions.

2010
MARS LANDER

Between 2001 and 2005, four more exploratory probes and robotic landers will be sent to Mars.

During the same period, TransHab, a manned lander module, will be assembled at the international space station and tested for a three-year return trip to Mars.

The 3.4m (11 ft) wide module will house six astronauts in accommodation on three levels. Several support landers, to provide supplies for a 600-day expedition and propulsion for the return journey, will be sent in advance of the planned landing in 2010.

This mission will mark the first time human beings have stepped onto another planet.

Technology Calendar

Science and technology are driving much of the change depicted in this atlas and will continue to transform our lives. This calendar looks at some of the main areas of research, identifies new developments, and predicts the most likely date of first application.

Occasionally the dates below differ from predictions elsewhere in the atlas that come from a different source. Experts in the same field often disagree on the significance of barriers and breakthroughs. Although we can predict accurately when the sun will rise tomorrow, very few other predictions will turn out to be as precise.

Earth

THE ENVIRONMENT

• effective prediction of some major natural disasters, such as earthquakes	2010
• deep underground cities in Japan	2020
• carbon dioxide fixation technologies to reduce global warming	2030
• artificial rain induction	2035

People

TELEMEDICINE AND BODY SHOPPING

• artificial muscle to assist weak hearts	1999
• artificial pancreas	1999
• artificial blood	2000
• disability assistance devices work by thought recognition	2000
• full personal medical records stored on smart card	2000
• artificial ears	2000
• electronic implants to stimulate muscles in disabled people	2002
• personal, wearable health monitors	2005
• human DNA base fully determined	2005
• synthetic retinal implants for simple vision	2005
• nanodevices roam and repair blood vessels	2010
• genetic screening widely used	2010
• artificial heart	2010
• individual's genome part of their medical record	2015
• artificial lungs	2015
• artificial kidneys	2015
• artificial brain cells	2017
• artificial liver	2020
• average lifespan in the rich world is 100 years	2020

Source: BT, Technology Calendar 1997–2045, 1997

• understanding of genetic, chemical, and physiological bases of behavior	2025
• artificial brain implants	2025
• artificial peripheral nerves	2025
• smart computers enhance human knowledge	2025
• artificial legs	2030
• fully-functioning artificial eyes	2030
• portable, permanently-connected brain "add-ons"	2033
• fully-functioning computer emulation of human brain	2035

HUMAN-MACHINE INTERFACE

• speech dialling: "Computer, call Susan"	2000
• tactile sensors comparable to human senses	2004
• odor and flavor sensors comparable to human senses	2005
• full-voice interaction with machine	2005
• voice synthesis comparable to human voice	2005
• portable translation device for simple conversation	2007
• household access by facial recognition	2010
• artificial senses via computer link to biological organs	2018
• odor and flavor sensors comparable to senses of a dog	2020
• thought recognition as everyday means of input	2025
• full, direct, two-way brain link	2030

ROBOTICS

• domestic robots: specialized, small, and cuddly	2005
• robotized space vehicles and facilities	2005
• fractal shape-changing robots (like robot Lego)	2005
• artificial insects and small animals with artificial brains	2005
• fire-fighting robots find and rescue people	2006
• totally automated factories with no people at all	2007
• anthropomorphic robots replace people in factories	2008
• robotic security and fire guards	2008
• housework robots fetch, carry, clean, tidy, and organize	2008
• fully mobile robotic pets	2010
• robotic mail delivery	2020
• robotic exercise companions	2020
• more robots than people in developed countries	2025

ENERGY

• solar cells more than 30% efficient	2000
• solar cells for residential power supply common	2000
• large area, amorphous solar cells more than 20% efficient	2001
• multi-layer solar cells above 50% efficient	2008
• water decomposition by sunlight	2015
• solar power stations in space	2030
• use of nuclear fusion as a power source	2040

GENETIC ENGINEERING

• chemicals from genetically engineered organisms, e.g. plastics from plants	2005
• entire human genome mapped	2006
• widespread genetic manipulation of plants and animals	2010

MATERIALS

• polymers with conductivity greater than copper at room temperature	2005
• smart clothes alter their own thermal properties	2007
• polymer gels for muscles, bioreactors, information processing	2010
• materials customized by manipulating individual atoms	2015
• intelligent materials with sensors, storage, and effectors	2015
• nanotechnology used in regular manufacturing	2015
• plants and toys based on nanotechnology	2015
• materials exhibit superconductivity at room temperature	2020
• smart skin for intelligent clothing and direct human repair	2020
• manufacture of long diamond fibers	2020
• antimatter produced, stored, and used to fuel space transport	2025

Source: BT, *Technology Calendar 1997–2045*, 1997

TELECOMMUNICATIONS

• worldwide low-earth-orbit satellite communications	1999
• analog neural network chips	1999
• evolving field programmable gate arrays	1999
• home and office cordless systems: optical wireless ceiling distribution node	2000
• optical inter-chip connection allows faster devices	2001
• go-anywhere personal numbers	2002
• global broadband fiber-based network	2005
• semiconductor devices based on 0.01 micron technology	2005
• use of wavelength division multiplexing in local access	2015

COMPUTING

• 1 Gigabit memory chip	1999
• self-recovering, multi-processing systems	2000
• 3-D opto-electronic integrated circuits	2002
• molecular computing	2003
• memory with access time of one nanosecond	2003
• use of quantum computing	2006
• 1 Terabit memory chip (1 million megabits)	2010
• DNA storage device	2010
• optical cards replace CD, VHS, audiotapes and magnetic disks	2007
• supercomputers with speed exceeding 1 ExaFLOPS	2010
• use of analog co-processors in PCs	2010
• DNA computer	2012
• chips using 10 billion transistors	2013
• office-automation systems use functions similar to brain	2016
• 1 Petabit memory chip (1 billion megabits)	2017
• intelligent computer imitates brain thought processes	2018
• molecular memory with density of 1 Terabyte per sq cm	2020
• parallel computer with 1 billion processors	2020

SURVEILLANCE AND SECURITY

• alarm systems for children in distress	1999
• wearable child-tracking devices	1999
• viruses based on artificial intelligence able to evolve and adapt	1999
• fire detection by odor or vibration	2002

Communications

MEDIA AND GADGETS

• refrigerator-front email based on cordless communications	1999
• LEFTEL flat screens 100 times sharper than 1997 LCDs	2000
• electronic newspapers	2000
• hand videophones	2000
• home shopping using barcode scanner or tablet	2000
• visual computer personalities on screens	2000
• selectable sound position	2001
• electronic notebooks with paper-quality contrast	2002
• personal display tablets for TV, magazines, etc.	2002
• one chip, multi-speaker voice recognition	2002
• hydraulic chairs for virtual reality games	2003
• virtual reality scenes for living areas at home	2005
• video walls: 2 meter single screens for life-size video meetings	2005
• active contact lens: lasers produce image directly on retina	2005
• holodeck meeting room with all walls, floor and ceiling covered in display	2010
• household access by facial recognition	2010
• 3-D TV without need for special glasses	2012
• holographic display	2015
• 3-D video conferencing	2015
• video recorders that can be programmed by adults	2018
• use of free-space holograms to convey 3-D images	2020

TRANSPORT

• interactive vehicle highway systems	2000
• integrated road traffic information systems	2003
• cryoplanes: hydrogen-fueled executive jets	2005
• cars powered by hydrogen fuel cells	2005
• ships with super-conductive electromagnetic thrust	2005
• ships able to navigate and dock automatically	2005
• car-trains: cars self-drive a few feet apart on smart highways	2015
• super-jumbos: flying-wing planes carry 1,000 passengers	2020

94

BUSINESS AND SOCIETY	
• information retrieval using natural language	1999
• virtual meeting places	1999
• information technology literacy needed for most jobs	2003
• electronic addictions common	2003
• real-time language translation for print and voice	2004
• electronic currency in use worldwide	2005
• electronic cash replaces paper money and coins	2005
• virtual reality widely used for job training and leisure	2005
• products increasingly customized	2005
• new housing manufactured in factories	2005
• anti-technology campaigns as people lose jobs	2008
• artificial intelligence used for strategic planning in business	2010
• personal banking replaced by software agents	2010
• most people in rich world are computer literate	2010
• electronic companies with minimum computer involvement	2012
• nomadic companies move around the internet to avoid taxes and debt	2015
• machine knowledge exceeds human knowledge	2017

NANOTECHNOLOGY	
• nanodevices roam and repair blood vessels	2010
• materials customized by manipulating individual atoms	2015
• nanotechnology used in regular manufacturiing	2015
• plants and toys based on nanotechnology	2015
• self-replicating nanomachines	2020
• nanoprobes to brain cells establish computer-to-brain link	2030

SPACE	
• low-cost, towed launch vessels	1999
• sub-orbital space tourism involves short periods of weightlessness	2002
• Next Generation Space Telescope (NGST)	2007
• antimatter produced, stored, and used to fuel space transport	2025
• construction of manned space laboratory begins	2030
• use of human hibernation in space travel	2030
• moon base the size of a small village	2040

Present and Future
World Table

World Table

Countries	1 Population		2 Life expectancy at birth		3 Water availability cubic meters per person	
	1995	**2050** *projected 1997*	**1995**	**2050** *projected 1997*	**1995**	**2050** *projected 1997*
Afghanistan	21,571,394	76,230,578	45.4	71.9	2,543	815
Albania	3,207,033	4,881,249	67.6	81.9	6,296	4,487
Algeria	28,539,321	58,879,809	68.0	79.5	527	251
Angola	10,069,501	34,578,614	46.3	73.4	17,012	4,730
Argentina	34,874,516	56,357,340	74.0	81.1	28,590	18,231
Armenia	3,463,914	3,956,140	69.3	80.9	3,654	3,032
Australia	18,079,330	22,846,538	79.2	83.8	19,198	13,565
Austria	7,988,416	7,069,773	76.4	83.9	11,224	12,153
Azerbaijan	7,616,038	10,339,783	64.7	79.9	4,379	3,031
Bahamas	256,616	326,812	72.1	80.9	–	–
Bahrain	575,925	1,097,951	73.0	83.0	162	96
Bangladesh	120,788,278	210,624,418	55.5	73.9	19,936	10,803
Barbados	256,394	275,761	74.2	80.9	192	163
Belarus	10,398,187	10,710,874	68.3	80.6	7,129	8,457
Belgium	10,136,118	8,976,085	77.0	83.9	1,234	1,280
Belize	214,061	489,105	68.3	77.5	75,117	33,333
Benin	5,522,677	22,171,075	52.2	73.3	4,770	1,426
Bhutan	1,780,638	4,935,375	51.0	72.2	53,672	18,326
Bolivia	7,357,610	15,240,486	59.3	79.2	40,464	17,682
Bosnia-Herzegovina	2,781,522	2,616,224	56.1	82.2	–	–
Botswana	1,452,586	2,051,001	47.6	77,2	10,138	4,428
Brazil	160,738,172	212,045,392	71.8	80.8	43,707	28,570
Brunei	292,266	705,130	71.2	77.7	–	–
Bulgaria	8,573,601	7,553,781	70.9	82.0	24,092	30,643
Burkina Faso	10,354,132	29,515,034	44.2	74.0	2,672	791
Burma	45,135,067	92,951,725	55.7	76.3	23,988	13,375
Burundi	5,924,312	18,554,557	49.7	74.5	24,594	213
Cambodia	10,561,373	37,300,574	49.5	73.9	49,691	23,282
Cameroon	13,851,774	48,083,024	52.9	74.5	20,315	6,388
Canada	28,510,708	37,086,480	78.9	83.7	98,667	79,803
Cape Verde	381,452	545,012	69.1	82.2	777	347
Central African Rep.	3,213,052	7,865,118	46.5	75.5	48,139	17,164
Chad	6,784,459	22,503,896	47.2	66.0	6,788	2,388
Chile	14,152,459	18,333,405	74.3	81.9	32,935	21,067
China	1,198,062,729	1,397,558,825	69.3	80.8	2,295	1,846
Colombia	36,200,251	55,798,204	72.5	82.3	29,877	17,179
Congo	2,472,752	5,856,433	45.8	75.4	320,864	95,314
Congo Dem. Rep.	45,430,619	182,567,278	46.4	74.1	83,634	6,189
Costa Rica	3,391,390	6,320,825	75.6	80.1	27,745	13,764
Côte d'Ivoire	14,149,113	42,346,789	45.6	75.0	5,674	2,451
Croatia	4,968,874	4,062,811	72.7	82.1	13,629	15,385
Cuba	10,901,673	10,565,056	74.9	80.6	3,147	3,057
Cyprus	736,261	1,058,493	76.0	83.2	1,208	875

Sources: **Cols 1 and 2:** US Bureau of the Census. **Col 3:** Population Action International, Washington DC. **Col 4:** International Food Policy Research Institute (IFPRI), Washington DC. **Col 5:** *World Bank Atlas 1997*. Ian Pearson, Network Wizards, http://www.nw.com/zone/WWW/top.html. **Col 6:** International Labour Organisation (ILO), Geneva. A dash signifies data not available.

4 Mainline telephones per 100 people		5 Internet connections		6 Work paid workforce, thousands		Countries
1995	2000 projected 1997	per 100,000 people July 1997	percentage growth Jan – July 1997	1995	2010 projected 1997	
0.2	0.2	–	–	8,376	13,523	Afghanistan
0.12	–	107	35%	1,654	1,978	Albania
4	5.0	31	11%	8,666	15,514	Algeria
6	45.0	18	350%	4,964	8,085	Angola
16	26.7	57,530	100%	13,512	18,704	Argentina
15.6	16.4	535	105%	1,749	2,143	Armenia
51	56.9	744,854	36%	9,026	10,556	Australia
47	52.8	92,987	-4%	3,750	3,968	Austria
8.5	8.3	231	1,829%	3,228	4,207	Azerbaijan
28.3	29.2	216	-68%	146	194	Bahamas
24	30.8	1,211	-6%	247	347	Bahrain
2	20.0	–	–	58,522	84,250	Bangladesh
34.5	36.7	23	-31%	135	151	Barbados
19	23.6	578	52%	5,335	5,564	Belarus
45.7	53.1	90,649	33%	4,180	4,198	Belgium
13.4	19.5	43	168%	70	115	Belize
0.5	0.8	13	44%	2,411	3,874	Benin
0.6	3.6	1	–	866	1,257	Bhutan
3.5	4.7	708	33%	2,973	4,410	Bolivia
7.1	–	87	3%	1,641	2,066	Bosnia-Herzegovina
4	7.6	238	892%	638	917	Botswana
7.5	8.9	88,058	-18%	72,384	89,282	Brazil
24	42.4	257	25%	127	187	Brunei
33.5	44.5	6,128	43%	4,312	4,021	Bulgaria
0.3	0.5	48	4,700%	5,286	7,616	Burkina Faso
0.3	–	6	–	23,621	31,683	Burma
0.3	0.9	9	–	3,221	5,062	Burundi
0.1	0.1	12	–	5,185	7,565	Cambodia
0.4	0.5	75	–	5,334	8,272	Cameroon
59	60.5	852,242	20%	15,621	17,511	Canada
5.7	14.8	16	–	151	246	Cape Verde
0.2	0.2	6	0%	1,589	2,168	Central African Rep.
0.1	0.1	–	–	3,052	4,511	Chad
13.2	26.8	21,782	19%	5,622	7,590	Chile
3	15.0	79,981	78%	729,128	826,824	China
10	13.3	14,691	2%	14,964	21,193	Colombia
0.8	0.9	7	–	1,073	1,655	Congo
0.1	0.1	9	–	19,196	29,597	Congo Dem. Rep.
16.4	28.9	5,834	34%	1,331	1,919	Costa Rica
0.8	1.1	276	21%	5,393	7,964	Côte d'Ivoire
27	42.1	7,368	34%	2,111	2,084	Croatia
3.2	3.2	86	358%	5,266	5,930	Cuba
47.4	64.2	2,268	32%	357	428	Cyprus

World Table

Countries	1 Population		2 Life expectancy at birth		3 Water availability cubic meters per person	
	1995	2050 projected 1997	1995	2050 projected 1997	1995	2050 projected 1997
Czech Republic	10,324,557	8,993,571	73.6	82.1	5,671	6,790
Denmark	5,228,717	4,831,197	77.2	83.9	2,489	2,484
Djibouti	421,320	1,329,419	49.7	72.6	3,827	1,527
Dominican Republic	7,948,223	13,459,330	68.7	80.5	2,557	1,522
Ecuador	11,242,435	20,815,132	70.7	81.8	27,400	14,818
Egypt	62,359,623	117,735,755	61.1	75.0	936	503
El Salvador	5,481,233	10,813,591	68.5	81.2	3,347	1,668
Equatorial Guinea	420,293	1,393,582	52.6	74.0	75,000	26,224
Eritrea	3,334,489	13,101,736	50.0	66.4	2,775	999
Estonia	1,477,796	1,300,188	68.0	80.5	11,828	16,236
Ethiopia	55,588,339	180,948,909	47.1	66.4	1,950	517
Fiji	772,891	1,284,973	65.4	76.7	36,416	20,495
Finland	5,099,117	4,387,825	75.3	83.9	22,126	21,848
France	58,118,981	54,797,593	78.4	84.0	3,408	3,392
Gabon	1,155,749	2,517,913	55.1	75.4	152,416	55,556
Gambia	1,162,544	4,037,592	52.5	74.5	7,201	3,072
Georgia	5,281,313	5,345,901	68.0	80.3	–	–
Germany	82,947,817	74,679,922	75.8	83.9	2,096	2,459
Ghana	17,290,791	34,324,026	55.9	71.4	3,068	1,039
Greece	10,494,142	9,335,495	77.9	83.9	5,610	6,507
Guatemala	10,998,602	25,147,162	64.9	79.4	10,922	3,952
Guinea	7,164,573	20,034,447	44.6	70.9	30,752	9,863
Guinea Bissau	1,124,537	2,970,216	47.9	70.3	25,257	10,097
Guyana	718,899	701,561	61.0	74.1	290,361	194,512
Haiti	6,433,855	12,345,249	49.0	68.5	1,544	628
Honduras	5,459,743	12,528,026	68.1	81.0	11,213	4,555
Hong Kong	6,187,972	7,574,483	82.0	83.9	–	–
Hungary	10,072,312	8,140,391	68.9	81.9	11,874	15,554
Iceland	268,081	354,205	79.9	83.9	624,535	462,810
India	936,461,577	1,564,236,902	59.3	77.3	2,244	1,360
Indonesia	203,459,288	330,566,219	61.2	78.0	12,813	7,949
Iran	64,625,455	142,335,748	67.0	80.6	1,719	690
Iraq	20,643,769	85,536,508	66.5	78.6	5,434	1,946
Ireland	3,570,949	3,458,018	75.4	83.9	14,100	13,127
Israel	8,384,141	13,647,303	77.8	83.1	389	235
Italy	57,383,872	54,544,465	77.9	83.9	2,919	3,967
Jamaica	2,573,833	3,712,026	74.7	82.2	3,363	2,136
Japan	125,200,170	102,010,452	79.4	82.9	4,374	4,993
Jordan	4,100,709	11,361,801	72.3	80.1	318	103
Kazakhstan	16,949,923	20,823,288	63.9	77.8	10,073	7,610
Kenya	27,616,268	45,061,285	56.9	77.4	1,112	457
Kirgistan	4,533,759	8,839,998	63.7	77.8	13,834	8,591
Korea (North)	23,486,550	33,710,614	70.1	79.3	3,032	2,038

Sources: **Cols 1 and 2:** US Bureau of the Census; **Col 3:** Population Action International, Washington DC; **Col 4:** International Food Policy Research Institute (IFPRI), Washington DC; **Col 5:** *World Bank Atlas 1997*, Ian Pearson, Network Wizards, http://www.nw.com/zone/WWW/top.html; **Col 6:** International Labour Organisation (ILO), Geneva. A dash signifies data not available.

4 Mainline telephones per 100 people		5 Internet connections		6 Work paid workforce, thousands		Countries
1995	2000 projected 1997	per 100,000 people July 1997	percentage growth Jan – July 1997	1995	2010 projected 1997	
23.6	35.3	50,623	19%	5,600	5,520	Czech Republic
61.3	66.4	159,312	45%	2,942	2,752	Denmark
1.3	1.5	9	–	–	–	Djibouti
7.9	13.0	109	-99%	3,290	4,652	Dominican Republic
6.1	7.9	1,540	54%	4,250	6,483	Ecuador
4.6	6.4	2,015	16%	22,509	34,179	Egypt
5.3	11.7	270	90%	2,296	3,651	El Salvador
0.6	1.2	5	–	167	245	Equatorial Guinea
0.5	–	1	0%	1,584	2,476	Eritrea
27.7	37.6	7,547	-25%	812	778	Estonia
0.2	0.2	–	–	24,642	38,785	Ethiopia
8.4	12.2	–	–	293	456	Fiji
55	56.5	409,702	26%	2,602	2,463	Finland
55.8	62.9	314,082	20%	25,859	27,133	France
3	5.0	–	–	508	697	Gabon
1.8	4.6	0	–	567	783	Gambia
9.6	9.3	392	72%	2,650	2,804	Georgia
49.3	60.6	912,116	23%	40,882	41,368	Germany
0.4	0.5	377	86%	8,125	12,829	Ghana
49.3	62.5	24,335	25%	4,422	4,629	Greece
2.7	3.6	1,242	104%	3,777	6,445	Guatemala
0.2	0.2	2	0%	3,525	4,958	Guinea
0.9	1.4	10	–	504	679	Guinea Bissau
5.3	17.6	98	34%	346	461	Guyana
0.8	0.9	0	–	3,153	4,132	Haiti
2.9	4.9	621	48%	2,021	3,496	Honduras
53	64.7	55,295	5%	3,169	3,446	Hong Kong
18.5	36.4	35,977	15%	4,746	4,410	Hungary
55.5	60.2	14,442	19%	150	174	Iceland
1.3	2.8	5,919	57%	402,110	538,367	India
1.7	4.8	12,484	15%	91,305	125,439	Indonesia
7.9	16.0	6	100%	20,362	36,543	Iran
3.3	2.9	0	–	5,364	9,106	Iraq
36.5	47.4	34,053	22%	1,414	1,641	Ireland
41.8	50.1	71,929	63%	2,297	3,260	Israel
43.4	48.5	230,398	34%	25,265	24,546	Italy
11.6	29.9	831	10%	1,262	1,590	Jamaica
48.7	53.8	1,073,807	35%	66,802	66,404	Japan
7.3	7.1	258	49%	1,523	2,774	Jordan
11.8	17.4	1,402	41%	8,004	9,237	Kazakhstan
0.9	1.0	471	55%	13,531	20,879	Kenya
7.3	7.5	117	–	1,865	2,382	Kirgistan
4.7	6.1	–	–	22,009	26,754	Korea (North)

World Table

Countries	Population		Life expectancy at birth		Water availability cubic meters per person	
	1995	**2050** projected 1997	**1995**	**2050** projected 1997	**1995**	**2050** projected 1997
Korea (South)	45,017,811	52,624,724	72.9	82.6	1,472	1,268
Kuwait	1,817,397	4,124,167	75.6	82.8	95	47
Laos	4,837,237	13,843,859	52.2	75.1	55,305	19,440
Latvia	2,506,569	2,065,583	66.6	80.4	13,407	17,980
Lebanon	3,695,921	7,712,775	69.7	80.5	1,854	1,075
Lesotho	1,933,082	3,692,208	52.5	75.6	2,565	921
Liberia	2,281,914	10,992,106	58.2	76.2	109,279	23,305
Libya	5,248,401	27,036,414	64.3	78.8	111	31
Lithuania	3,661,469	3,523,604	67.7	80.6	6,478	7,340
Luxembourg	409,385	466,067	77.7	83.9	12,285	10,846
Macedonia	2,094,313	2,152,502	71.8	82.0	–	–
Madagascar	13,288,948	48,327,070	51.8	69.6	22,657	6,633
Malawi	9,445,827	14,787,877	37.2	72.7	1,933	627
Malaysia	19,549,627	39,742,880	69.5	80.2	22,642	11,972
Mali	9,375,132	43,296,071	46.4	71.4	6,207	1,820
Malta	371,774	460,082	77.6	83.9	82	68
Marshall Islands	56,157	348,080	63.5	77.1	–	–
Mauritania	2,263,202	9,301,068	48.5	72.6	5,013	1,876
Mauritius	1,128,211	1,613,967	70.3	78.0	1,970	1,330
Mexico	93,985,848	170,280,019	73.3	82.6	3,921	2,319
Moldova	4,459,435	5,324,919	65.0	80.0	3,088	2,666
Mongolia	2,453,944	4,057,444	60.4	75.6	9,988	4,934
Morocco	29,168,848	58,374,712	69.0	82.9	1,131	635
Mozambique	17,150,437	47,805,294	43.8	72.2	12,051	4,017
Namibia	1,628,854	6,003,605	64.1	79.5	29,622	10,919
Nepal	21,560,869	58,970,861	53.1	76.2	7,923	3,170
Netherlands	15,478,038	14,283,378	77.6	83.9	5,813	6,018
New Zealand	3,507,617	4,561,165	76.7	82.9	91,828	62,038
Nicaragua	4,158,735	9,714,373	65.3	80.5	42,445	17,638
Niger	8,843,901	33,895,881	40.2	68.0	3,552	940
Nigeria	100,785,018	386,338,789	54.0	79.2	2,506	827
Norway	4,362,046	4,131,176	77.4	83.9	90,489	83,511
Oman	2,110,323	8,644,420	70.3	80.1	874	177
Pakistan	126,404,163	260,244,948	58.1	71.9	3,435	1,310
Panama	2,608,789	4,418,367	73.9	80.9	54,732	32,990
Papua New Guinea	4,294,750	10,049,378	56.9	74.8	186,236	83,117
Paraguay	5,358,198	14,185,796	73.6	81.8	65,037	24,990
Peru	24,094,221	38,013,641	68.7	81.6	1,700	946
Philippines	72,859,889	150,271,797	65.7	75.5	4,761	2,475
Poland	38,589,294	38,705,258	72.0	82.0	1,458	1,415
Portugal	9,864,697	8,754,750	75.1	83.9	7,091	7,999
Qatar	615,125	1,881,703	72.9	82.5	91	58
Romania	21,924,216	18,103,574	69.3	81.9	9,152	10,942

Sources: **Cols 1 and 2:** US Bureau of the Census; **Col 3:** Population Action International, Washington DC; **Col 4:** International Food Policy Research Institute (IFPRI), Washington DC; **Col 5:** World Bank Atlas 1997; Ian Pearson; Network Wizards. http://www.nw.com/zone/WWW/top.html; **Col 6:** International Labour Organisation (ILO), Geneva. A dash signifies data not available.

4 Mainline telephones per 100 people		5 Internet connections per 100,000	percentage	6 Work paid workforce, thousands		Countries
1995	2000 projected 1997	people July 1997	growth Jan – July 1997	1995	2010 projected 1997	
41.5	55.6	181,329	116%	11,716	13,880	Korea (South)
23	34.1	4,617	31%	621	1,135	Kuwait
0.4	0.8	0	0%	2,363	3,666	Laos
28	33.8	6,562	32%	1,376	1,269	Latvia
8.2	8.1	1,226	100%	1,001	1,504	Lebanon
0.6	1.4	16	1500%	823	1,245	Lesotho
0.2	–	0	–	893	1,727	Liberia
5.9	–	4	–	1,545	2,578	Libya
25.4	30.9	2,876	54%	1,920	1,943	Lithuania
56.5	66.1	4,818	-1%	175	187	Luxembourg
16.5	–	471	33%	985	1,129	Macedonia
0.2	0.1	41	52%	6,948	11,385	Madagascar
0.4	0.5	–	–	4,689	6,821	Malawi
16.6	31.0	49,430	59%	8,042	12,079	Malaysia
0.2	0.4	29	93%	5,308	8,238	Mali
45.9	58.5	1,033	52%	136	151	Malta
5.7	29.5	3	300%	–	–	Marshall Islands
0.4	0.5	0	–	1,042	1,535	Mauritania
13.1	33.0	211	73%	470	573	Mauritius
9.6	14.0	48,942	12%	35,672	50,695	Mexico
13.1	16.2	215	78%	2,166	2,404	Moldova
3.2	3.4	17	70%	1,185	1,791	Mongolia
4.3	11.6	1,138	67%	10,215	14,788	Morocco
0.3	0.3	60	-36%	8,991	13,175	Mozambique
5.1	7.0	361	28%	634	912	Namibia
0.4	0.5	172	166%	9,898	14,730	Nepal
52.5	59.4	352,124	26%	7,218	7,296	Netherlands
47.9	52.5	197,061	84%	1,775	2,113	New Zealand
2.3	4.1	874	42%	1,578	2,687	Nicaragua
0.1	0.1	34	580%	4,353	7,045	Niger
0.4	0.5	7	14%	44,193	68,613	Nigeria
55.6	61.5	213,300	18%	2,224	2,312	Norway
7.7	8.6	–	–	599	1,096	Oman
1.6	3.2	1,572	94%	49,504	82,115	Pakistan
11.4	14.6	709	-28%	1,067	1,470	Panama
1	1.3	239	23839%	2,109	2,965	Papua New Guinea
3.1	3.7	771	288%	1,770	2,817	Paraguay
4.7	8.5	7,233	18%	8,387	12,715	Peru
2.1	4.4	8,449	72%	27,855	40,174	Philippines
14.8	25.5	50,447	-12%	19,239	20,576	Poland
36.1	53.6	23,265	-20%	4,907	4,903	Portugal
22.3	26.3	507	1519%	304	362	Qatar
13.1	16.8	9,088	-8%	10,647	10,744	Romania

World Table

Countries	1 Population		2 Life expectancy at birth		3 Water availability cubic meters per person	
	1995	2050 projected 1997	1995	2050 projected 1997	1995	2050 projected 1997
Russia	142,291,368	142,886,927	63.2	80.3	30,298	39,346
Rwanda	6,017,568	18,927,543	36.2	74.3	1,215	372
Saudi Arabia	18,729,576	97,119,774	68.5	82.5	249	76
Senegal	8,790,420	39,689,503	56.1	75.4	4,740	1,681
Seychelles	76,970	95,731	68.9	81.0	–	–
Sierra Leone	4,589,259	18,369,471	46.9	74.3	38,141	14,075
Singapore	3,332,875	4,589,225	77.9	83.6	180	143
Slovakia	5,356,518	5,591,087	72.9	82.1	5,770	5,858
Slovenia	1,956,569	1,513,035	75.0	82.2	–	–
Solomon Islands	399,206	1,157,823	70.8	81.2	118,254	37,500
Somalia	9,164,988	32,545,779	55.1	72.8	1,422	371
South Africa	40,967,113	53,442,005	59.6	77.0	1,206	547
Spain	39,117,865	33,832,753	78.1	83.9	2,809	3,505
Sri Lanka	18,342,660	24,154,460	72.1	80.2	2,410	1,600
Sudan	30,556,356	93,624,886	54.7	74.1	5,766	2,569
Suriname	429,544	709,549	69.8	80.1	468,384	281,294
Swaziland	966,977	4,754,297	56.8	75.7	5,251	2,020
Sweden	8,846,542	8,523,398	77.9	83.9	20,482	18,801
Switzerland	7,163,877	6,734,471	77.5	83.9	6,977	7,210
Syria	15,086,586	43,463,336	66.8	78.4	3,780	1,558
Taiwan	21,274,236	24,817,147	75.7	83.9	–	–
Tajikistan	5,831,240	16,958,038	64.3	78.0	17,382	8,192
Tanzania	28,568,877	64,556,146	43.0	74.7	2,964	1,000
Thailand	58,240,930	69,740,733	68.4	80.8	3,073	2,453
Togo	4,410,370	20,725,195	57.4	76.6	2,938	948
Trinidad & Tobago	1,271,159	1,446,600	70.1	77.2	3,963	2,686
Tunisia	8,856,484	15,723,279	62.4	81.0	434	245
Turkey	61,437,246	103,648,860	71.5	82.9	3,174	1,972
Turkmenistan	4,074,635	9,321,458	61.3	77.6	17,669	9,096
Uganda	19,730,436	53,886,447	40.9	73.4	3,352	995
Ukraine	51,088,930	45,833,480	66.6	80.4	4,463	5,661
United Arab Emirates	2,181,279	4,057,458	74.0	82.5	902	543
United Kingdom	58,360,677	54,312,998	76.2	83.9	1,222	1,209
United States	263,168,332	394,240,528	75.9	82.0	9,277	7,130
Uruguay	3,216,380	4,255,989	74.7	82.8	38,920	30,792
Uzbekistan	22,983,820	55,249,628	64.5	77.9	5,694	2,874
Venezuela	21,564,471	37,772,517	71.8	81.3	60,291	31,244
Vietnam	72,814,642	119,463,548	66.7	79.7	5,095	2,898
Western Sahara	217,211	572,433	46.3	–	–	–
Yemen	13,011,934	55,178,738	58.9	81.7	346	85
Yugoslavia	10,573,569	10,307,979	73.5	82.0	–	–
Zambia	8,968,944	23,563,947	37.1	71.0	14,355	5,281
Zimbabwe	11,160,864	14,656,688	42.9	79.6	1,787	803

Sources: **Cols 1 and 2:** US Bureau of the Census. **Col 3:** Population Action International, Washington DC. **Col 4:** International Food Policy Research Institute (IFPRI), Washington DC. **Col 5:** *World Bank Atlas 1997*. Ian Pearson, Network Wizards. http://www.nw.com/zone/WWW/top.html. **Col 6:** International Labour Organisation (ILO), Geneva. A dash signifies data not available.

4 Mainline telephones per 100 people		5 Internet connections		6 Work paid workforce, thousands		Countries
1995	2000 projected 1997	per 100,000 people July 1997	percentage growth Jan – July 1997	1995	2010 projected 1997	
17	20.6	86,281	53%	77,193	78,422	Russia
0.2	0.4	7	–	2,737	5,424	Rwanda
9.6	11.8	371	–	5,953	9,917	Saudi Arabia
1	1.7	387	299%	3,707	5,551	Senegal
17.8	24.8	35	–	–	1,947	Seychelles
0.4	0.5	–	–	1,559	2,322	Sierra Leone
47.8	58.6	72,231	113%	1,687	1,852	Singapore
20.8	32.3	12,743	29%	2,812	3,031	Slovakia
30.9	45.3	17,582	21%	964	930	Slovenia
1.7	2.1	4	-20%	195	306	Solomon Islands
2	20.0	–	–	4,130	6,782	Somalia
9.5	10.4	122,370	20%	16,205	23,199	South Africa
38.5	45.9	135,359	12%	16,914	17,654	Spain
1.1	6.1	736	81%	7,501	9,688	Sri Lanka
0.3	0.5	2	–	10,340	15,496	Sudan
13	18.6	0	−100%	153	223	Suriname
2.1	2.6	240	-29%	304	493	Swaziland
68	67.7	305,890	18%	4,757	4,784	Sweden
61.3	64.0	164,476	13%	3,830	4,126	Switzerland
6.3	9.7	0	–	4,209	7,595	Syria
43	–	99,283	52%	–	–	Taiwan
4.5	4.5	–	–	2,168	3,520	Tajikistan
0.3	0.3	69	2196%	15,413	22,965	Tanzania
5.9	14.5	14,216	41%	34,474	39,718	Thailand
0.5	0.8	6	20%	1,690	2,585	Togo
16	19.2	961	200%	536	723	Trinidad & Tobago
65.8	–	75	92%	3,351	5,030	Tunisia
21.2	37.1	33,769	61%	27,883	37,523	Turkey
7.6	9.6	2	–	1,702	2,555	Turkmenistan
0.2	0.2	28	50%	9,854	14,914	Uganda
15.7	18.1	12,515	38%	25,825	25,865	Ukraine
28.3	29.6	2,191	12%	1,106	1,386	United Arab Emirates
50.2	56.0	1,155,546	60%	28,907	29,152	United Kingdom
62.7	72.0	15,646,597	23.5%	135,406	154,249	United States
19.6	28.7	1,422	-47%	1,429	1,639	Uruguay
7.6	8.5	235	45%	9,229	14,109	Uzbekistan
11.1	16.0	6,684	110%	8,511	12,921	Venezuela
1.1	12.1	4	-28%	37,501	49,893	Vietnam
–	–	–	–	–	–	Western Sahara
1.2	1.3	3	-42%	4,752	8,349	Yemen
19.1	22.7	3,037	5%	4,815	5,125	Yugoslavia
0.8	0.8	283	51%	3,347	5,216	Zambia
1.4	1.5	324	31%	5,168	7,408	Zimbabwe

Commentaries

The Future of the Earth

In the futures presented in this first section of the atlas, the countries of the world are interdependent. Experiences will be shared on a regional or even global scale. As with many other predictions of the future, the widespread impact predicted for global warming (see pages 18–19) makes assumptions about human behavior and our ability to change. It cannot take into account completely new technologies that may be developed to counter climate change. Perhaps such predictions can themselves be the necessary catalyst and enable us to change a future we do not want to accept.

We are unlikely to change the future of the universe, but cosmology is taking dramatic leaps forward in the understanding of its fate. When we look into the night sky we look backward in time. Powerful space telescopes, such as the Hubble, can look backward billions of years. The Next Generation Space Telescope (see **Space Exploration**, pages 88–9) expected by 2007, will be even more powerful than the Hubble. Such telescopes provide new clues as to the structure of the universe and how it was formed, and since the first second in the life of the universe may be echoed in its final moments, they also provide vital new clues as to its future.

The various scenarios predicted for the future of the universe (see pages 10–11) show how many big questions remain unanswered. The illustrations use logarithmic scales, in which each factor of ten is given the same distance along an axis. Such scales are often used in science where very wide ranges are involved. Here, it becomes possible to show the tiniest fraction of a second in the very early life of the universe together with alternatives for its long-term future.

The earth will vanish long before the end of the universe. Our sun will last about another five billion years before entering what is called the giant red phase, during which time it will expand, burning up the earth.

Billions of years before this, a direct strike on earth by an asteroid or comet as small as 10–50 km in diameter could wreak havoc (see **Spaceguard**, pages 12–13). Mass destruction and even human extinction are possible. The risk of such a collision in any particular year is small. But asteroid 1997XF11 will just miss the earth in 2028, an asteroid thought to be a quarter the size of the one which wiped out the dinosaurs. No adequate protection exists yet against possible collisions, but methods of evasive action are beginning to be developed. The technology currently available involves shooting missiles at them, perhaps even a hydrogen bomb or other nuclear missile. But asteroids and comets only a few kilometers across weigh billions of tons and travel at thousands of miles per hour. Blowing an asteroid to pieces in a massive explosion may serve to spread the damage over an even wider area. A less dangerous strategy would be to push it along slowly, thereby deflecting it from its path.

Much smaller pieces of debris are left in orbit, deliberately or by accident, by space missions. Such debris may be small but it travels faster than any bullet and could be a hazard to future space missions. The technology required to remove space junk will be relatively less sophisticated. Shooting lasers at it or catching it in nets may turn out to be realistic solutions.

As earthquakes and volcanoes slowly rearrange the earth's surface, they can cause untold misery and loss of life, especially within densely packed cities. In the future it may be possible to predict such disasters and, with the benefit of early warnings, dramatically reduce the damage they inflict, but the necessary technology has yet to be developed. After an initial earthquake or volcanic eruption, tilt meters and seismology can only help to predict further activity a few hours, or at most days, ahead.

The past activity of volcanoes and earthquakes (see **Faultlines**, pages 14–15) follows the very slight but constant movement of the earth's tectonic plates. Here again the future is predicted to mimic the past. Two hundred million years into the future, the movement together of the continents can be compared with the shape of the ancient continent of Gondwanaland.

There are other potential long-term challenges. **Sea Change** (see pages 16–17) predicts that the next ice age will begin in 100,000 years. By then we human beings may have acquired the capacity to manage our earth and environment. Or will we have created so many problems here that we have left earth and migrated elsewhere?

The threat of global warming is much closer at hand. Carbon dioxide already in the atmosphere seems to be changing the earth's climate. Major weather changes could wreak havoc, particularly for agriculture. If in the future the polar ice caps were to melt completely, a great deal of land – especially coastal regions and small islands – could disappear under the sea.

The changes to the ozone layer of the earth's atmosphere (see **Ozone**, pages 20–21) show that a disaster once predicted may indeed by averted. The ozone hole was first discovered over Antarctica in the 1980s and was found to be caused by chlorofluorocarbons widely used in refrigeration and aerosols. Although for decades it will remain a human health risk, as a result of international commitment to use alternative chemicals it is currently forecast to close up by 2060.

The Future of People

Population growth is often deemed the source of humankind's ultimate Armageddon. The world's population is expected to double by 2050 (see pages 24–5), but official estimates of the rate of population growth are now being revised downward.

Part of the population explosion is accounted for by the fact that people are living longer. In the rich world, the decline in population growth means there will be fewer young people to support increasingly elderly populations. The growth of spare-part surgery provides hints of a synthetic future for human beings, when some people may attempt to live forever.

More than ever we will live in close contact in towns and cities and enjoy the benefits of international travel. Consequently, we will be exposed to many more diseases and will be more likely to carry diseases across the world. In addition, as we eliminate tropical forests we are increasing the evolution rates of many species of bugs that may become new sources of human disease. Overzealous use of antibiotics, even putting them into animal feed, has caused the evolution of new strains of antibiotic-resistant bugs. Though we may be winning many battles against infectious disease, some diseases may learn to resist available cures. Some people with infectious diseases such as tuberculosis fail to finish their course of treatment, expose others and encourage development of antibiotic-resistant TB bugs. Some bugs may mutate beyond our ability to treat them.

Biological warfare is always a serious potential threat to human health (see **Military Might**, pages 80–1). So, too, is the nightmarish possibility of genetic engineering gone wrong. As we tinker with the very stuff of life, we may be playing with fire, able to burn ourselves badly without fully understanding how to control it.

Changes in diet mean that all over the world people are getting taller, but we are also suffering more often from diseases and ailments resulting from our lifestyles. Tobacco is set to kill far more people in the future, mostly in poor countries. Drug research, medicine, and technology may offer an increasing range of solutions but will not be universally available.

Telemedicine, which allows doctors to be effectively present elsewhere, even right across the planet, will for a long time benefit only the few. Using telemedicine and through virtual reality, a doctor will be able to operate in real time, manipulating instruments from a distance. It takes the same time for a nerve signal to move from a surgeon's fingertip to the brain as it does for a signal to cross the Atlantic on an optical fiber.

Completely new medical methods may soon be available, as microscopic devices are created to maintain or repair our bodies from within (see **Nanotechnology**, pages 86–7). Borrowing ideas from nature, we may be able to use genetic engineering to build them.

The most exciting short-term goal is mapping the 100,000 genes in the human body. Once this is achieved, by about 2006, we can make use of a variety of technologies such as gene identification and detection chips to screen people for diseases they may be prone to develop. That could enable us to customize our lifestyles, minimize risks, and use our known gene profile to steer ourselves toward the diet most likely to maintain our health. In the future, some foods may themselves be custom products of genetic engineering designed to treat specific ailments (see **Food**, pages 48–9).

Each decade, there is a significant increase in the proportion of the human body that could be replaced by artificial body parts. For a few people this could become death by installments. By 2030, only the brain will remain irreplaceable and that represents only a few percent of human body weight.

We are a long way from creating an android, or a robot with a human appearance, that could be given a human brain. But there have been some quite surprising developments over the last few years. Already real, organic ears have been produced or cultured from human cells, in a special matrix that dissolves away when the ear is complete. We have since seen replacement breasts grown in the same way. Electronic cochlea implants into the inner ear have greatly improved quality of life for thousands of people. Electronic retinal implants will soon allow previously blind people to read large text. By 2020 artificial eyes may be available that are as good as the real thing.

After 2030, we will probably be able to make a link between our brains and external electronic devices such as computers. Initially this will be one way and based on thought recognition. But these future computers may one day act effectively as extensions of our brains, even able to take over some brain functions.

Research on artificial intelligence (see pages 36–7) suggests that a wholly artificial brain may be feasible by 2035. The best chance human beings have of immortality is to back up our minds before our bodies die. To extend the quality of immortality beyond being the memory inside a computer requires the development of androids. Although many of the required technologies already exist in embryonic form, it will be a long time before they can all be linked together to create such a creature.

As with other medical treatments, expectations of solutions to infertility are increasing. The advance of technology raises awkward questions. While there will undoubtedly be resistance to mass customization of babies, there are many gray areas where the ethical issues are complex.

The Future of Resources

Resource prediction is a difficult and controversial field. In the 1960s and 1970s, many predicted not only that we would run out of oil by the early 1990s, but that most metals would become scarce and shoot up in price. But technology and exploration have revealed new reserves, and for some potentially scarce materials substitutes have been found. In telecommunications, for instance, the problem of copper shortages was averted by the move to optical fiber cabling. To cable a whole country, the only raw materials needed are a few bucketsful of sand.

Organic resources, on the other hand, both living and fossil, do demand conservation. Maintaining the world's forests, the fauna and flora on land and at sea, and the gene pools they contain, is not just a matter of recycling.

There is now some managed reforestation in the developed world, but however useful this is, it will not replace the unique frontier forest being rapidly destroyed. A forest replanted with a few species of trees, and into which a few more species of plants and animals have been introduced, cannot replace rich and complex ecosystems such as ancient rainforests. Tropical and ancient forests house many biological chemical factories that in the future may provide invaluable drugs and other materials.

Most extinct species will never be recovered. Jurassic Park technology may eventually work for some highly valued species recently lost, but thousands of species are being lost each year, many more than we can ever hope to recreate. Many species are disappearing before they have even been discovered, so we may never know the extent of what has been lost.

Through genetic engineering, new species could be artificially created in laboratories. This new field raises major issues, such as human health and safety and the effect on the rest of the environment. Controls will be necessary but the time may soon come when custom-designed organisms can be routinely created.

Water (see pages 46–7) accounts for most of the world's surface, but fresh water accounts for only a tiny proportion of it. Renewable fresh water accounts for an even tinier proportion. As the population grows and living standards rise worldwide, so the demand for water will increase and more countries will face water shortages. Many predict that water could become a major cause of international friction between some countries. The technologies so far tried, such as desalination plants, or land and sea redistribution including the towing of icebergs, have not been particularly successful.

Food distribution is often a bigger problem than actual shortages. Fertilizers and pesticides have improved the natural yields of plants. Genetic engineering should facilitate further improvements. Plants will not only be made more productive, they will also be made more resistant to drought and pests. In the rich world, genetic engineering may be used to give medicinal properties to fruits and vegetables. Innovative experiments are being tested in desert areas to see whether artificial plants can capture their limited humidity for the soil, eventually making it possible to make a desert climate more hospitable to real plants.

As energy using non-renewable fuels is burned, carbon dioxide is emitted into the atmosphere. The increasing level of carbon dioxide emissions caused by burning fossil fuels is one of the main causes of global warming (see pages 18–19). Current energy forecasts (see pages 52–3) suggest that between 1993 and 2010 there will be a worldwide increase in consumption of almost 50 percent.

There are already a number of renewable, cleaner alternatives to fossil fuel burning and others are being researched. Within the next ten to fifteen years solar power should become as cheap as conventional electricity. Other renewable energy sources such as wind, tides and waves may in some ways be attractive, but can also be damaging to the environment. Turbine farms can visually destroy areas of natural beauty and tidal power in estuaries can destroy whole ecosystems. Sometime during the next century, we will be able to harness nuclear fusion as an energy source so long as we can devise the other technologies needed to make it completely safe. Few would challenge the need to protect the environment from the effects of growing energy consumption, but it is much harder to agree on what this means or how it can be done.

As space exploration develops, it may become possible to extract minerals, precious metals and water from asteroids and ship them back to earth. This may be science fiction today, but not tomorrow.

The Future of Communications

First the telephone changed the lives of millions. Then came the turn of computers. Now, communications and computing are fast converging. The internet, for example, is a communications network that already links almost 40 million computers. Communications and computer processing technologies are being incorporated into a wide range of consumer electronics to provide the final phase of an information technology revolution – mass access to digital multimedia.

Rapidly falling costs of communications, coupled with the multiplication of services available, will have a huge impact on every aspect of our lives over the coming years. Half of the world's people have yet to make their first phone call, but with the promise of vast returns, telecommunications companies are investing in systems that will reach the world over. Even before cables cover the more remote areas, new fleets of satellites will offer cheaper telecommunications on almost every corner. This will be especially valuable where the waiting time for conventional phones is very long. Roving business people from the rich world will want to stay in touch wherever they go and many parts of the developing world will benefit as a result.

Terrestrial mobile networks will allow people to keep in touch with each other more cheaply. Some of us will choose to avoid the trouble of installing a fixed line altogether. A new international mobile technology, UMTS (Universal Mobile Telecommunications Service), will soon give much faster rates of data transmission, so that waiting times for email and internet access on the move will be much shorter. Indeed, on all networks, voice calls will soon account for only a small proportion of all communications. Already most conversations on the planet are between machines.

Optical fiber will always provide the greatest capacity and speed. In the early 1990s, the most that could be squeezed down an optical cable was 2.5 billion bits per second. Yet by 2003, a worldwide network that is up to 400 times faster should be operational. However, even this falls far short of fiber's theoretical limits.

We cannot expect superhighway speed in homes or offices for many years, but change will still be rapid. As communications and computing converge, new services will become available. By 2001, a box that sits on top of our television sets will provide interactive digital television and electronic shopping, greatly increase the amount of information available on the internet, and allow us to wander through virtual reality environments with our friends. Such services would be delivered by satellite, cable networks, or over plain old telephone lines. A personal computer will no longer be needed to access these services, network capacity into homes will increase, and the long wait for an internet page should soon be a thing of the past. We are already seeing signs of new psychosocial problems of the future – internet addiction and escapism into cyberspace.

The internet is growing fast, but more than a third of all personal computers are now connected to it (see pages 58–9). Early explosive growth is showing signs of slowing down. But cheaper technology and faster networks may trigger another phase in which internet growth accelerates again. The more people are wired up, the more services will expand, perhaps pushing the internet close to saturation again in just a few years. As a result, sensible predictions of internet growth are impossible for more than a few months ahead.

As technology becomes cheaper, more powerful, and easier to drive access to information technology will be influenced more by choice and lifestyle. In the rich world, as with television, we will change from being "haves" or "have nots," and become "wants" or "don't wants." The process will inevitably be slower in the developing world, but the path will be similar. This is the beginning of an era in which our geographic location will be much less significant and in which the social, political and economic connections between people will become more and more global.

The wired world is facilitating other changes in our lives. Satellites can see objects on the ground only a few feet across; video cameras watch over many town and shopping centers; and traffic cameras attached to computers can recognize car number plates while capturing photographic evidence of the occupants. Surveillance can be beneficial when it reduces crime or the fear of crime in our neighborhoods. But governments can also use it to impose greater social and political controls and, given these extra powers, most countries do not have adequate privacy laws for the protection of their citizens.

In the future, cars will almost certainly convert to using fuel cells and electric motors. Given the vast increase expected in the number of vehicles on the roads, this will be essential for environmental reasons. In fact, information technology will by no means replace physical travel. Teletravel will whet our appetite for real travel. Teleworking will make travel for leisure and pleasure more inviting.

It will soon become possible to speak to your computer, telling it you would like to go to the theater. Having shown you a preview and confirmed your interest in a particular show, it will buy and print your tickets. At the appropriate time, it will book your car parking space, negotiate with traffic computers, book a route without traffic jams, and having assessed the likely duration of your journey, tell you when you need to leave. In your car, a navigation computer will guide you to the car park while you sit back and relax, enjoying a wider range of in-car entertainment, in almost guaranteed safety. This futuristic fantasy is probably only thirty years away.

The Future of Globalization

Developments in transportation and advanced telecommunications have already made the world much more accessible. Global travel for business or pleasure has become commonplace. Contact between cultures and political systems is already unprecedented and growing.

Tourism (see pages 68–9) is one of the world's fastest-growing industries. By 2010, to cope with the expected increase in passengers, there will be planes that hold a thousand people, with gymnasiums and jogging tracks on board. By 2015 or so, there will be near-earth space tours. They may cost tens of thousands of dollars for just a few hours in space, but they already have potential buyers. Soon after, there will be hotels in orbit, with a new generation of space planes ferrying guests to and fro. Space travelers, as well as admiring the view, will be able to take part in space walks and zero-gravity sports. Such holidays may cost upwards of $100,000 for a weekend, but there will be no shortage of takers. There are no dates yet for holidays on the moon, but these are only a matter of time.

Back on earth, a growing number of holiday destinations are suffering from severe congestion and other environmental pressures. In the future, restricted access will become standard for the world's most popular places. Instead we may have to resort to virtual visits over the internet. Already, a few cities in the USA have begun to recreate themselves in cyberspace, enabling the virtual visitor to wander around art galleries, for example, and see the main sights, all via the computer screen. As the technology improves, many of the world's great sights will become available via immersive virtual reality.

As new technologies increase productivity in just about every sphere, more work will be done by fewer people. By about 2012, robots should be available that are able to do just about any physical job. A few years later, computers should be able to do just about any mental job. These developments will begin to have a vast impact on employment. We will be forced to reconsider how we can all earn a living and what we really want out of life. The information economy may be followed by the care economy. In a care economy, many more people will be employed to do the jobs that require human interaction, the jobs that only people can do.

More and more transnational companies will encompass the world, in search of bigger markets, cheap resources and cheap labor, and additional sources of investment. There will also be a growing number of "virtual companies," which retain a small core of key workers, but hire everyone else on a contract or project-by-project basis.

The world is becoming increasingly urban. In developing countries, changes in agricultural production and higher living standards in cities mean that millions of rural dwellers are drawn there in search of work. The rich world is also becoming more urban. Although many have predicted that with the benefits of information technology we will all work from home and will be free to move to a quiet life away from town and city centers, relatively few of us will actually do so. Just as many will move into cities and towns. People are simply gregarious and cities offer many more exciting facilities.

Some parts of the information industry may become concentrated in specialist cities rather than stretch across the globe. In information technology it can, surprisingly, be advantageous to have computers close together. As computer processing speed increases, so the delays in sending data down a cable become relatively longer, a problem helped by reducing physical distance.

Political systems are changing too, undoubtedly aided by telecommunications. There are many different forms and levels of democracy, and greater political knowledge increases political pressures on the state. People living under the most highly oppressive regimes may be cut off from a world that could strengthen their will to push for additional freedoms.

Artificial intelligence may eventually have a major impact on political systems. The potential exists for democracy to become almost automated, taking individual preferences into account directly. An increasing number of policies and issues will have a direct effect on more than a single country. Eventually this may lead to pressures to allow international voting. Finally, as the internet and ultimately the global superhighway make geography less significant in every other area of life, we may see a move of power away from geographic domains toward groups linked by a whole range of similar values or interests. Such cybercommunities could be linked by instantaneous communication and become as large as some states. They may develop some of the trappings of states: acquiring leaders and governments and finding the means to control their membership. They may even come into conflict with other cybercommunities.

One of the main driving forces behind new technologies is still the pursuit of military advantage, as is shown in **Military Might** (see pages 80–1). The warriors of the far future may be as small as insects, but would have enough intelligence to do great harm. Some wars will be fought electronically in which the opponents have no need to travel beyond their own borders. Since electronic warfare necessitates neither enormous armies nor expenditure, terrorism may become a much bigger problem. As the developed world becomes increasingly dependent on computers, it will be increasingly vulnerable to assault across networks. Future warfare may have very different characteristics.

For the foreseeable future, most wars will be civil wars and will be fought with familiar weapons. But as globalization continues, international and regional alliances will become more important. **United Nations** (see pages 82–3) suggests that the UN may eventually achieve its original task of establishing a permanent global peacekeeping and security system.

Into the Unknown

Nanotechnology is often hailed as the most significant technology of the 21st century. It will gradually arrive over decades of research and development but we do already have some understanding of its far-reaching implications.

The central pillar of this potentially magic science is the ability to manipulate matter routinely at the atomic scale (see **Nanotechnology**, pages 86–7). If tiny machines could be built atom by atom, and these could in turn build replicas of themselves, atom by atom, then very soon we could move from having one machine to having billions of them. All we would need to provide is the raw materials.

Nanomachines could then be built that would themselves be able to build almost anything. We could make any food we choose by putting mud, water and air into a machine and using nanomachines to reassemble the appropriate atoms into the required form. Taking nanotechnology to its limits, factories could in effect be grown from a small seed containing building instructions and a few parents of a few species of nanomachines.

Nanotechnology machines could roam around our bodies repairing the damage they find. This would greatly enhance the body's natural repair systems and could postpone or even eliminate the effects of ageing. People who have their bodies or heads frozen on death believe that nanotechnology will either be able to repair the damage causing death, or will be able to copy information stored in their brains ready to be uploaded into an android at some later date. Such possibilities are highly debatable, but the prospect of billions of nanoprobes connected to every cell in a human brain does suggest that it will eventually be possible for the mind to be connected to a machine. Potential applications in the long-term would then range from telepathic communication with others across a network, super-intelligence via a transparent connection to ultra-smart computers, or even the potential to back up our minds in case of accidental death.

Biology continually manipulates atoms using a mixture of chemical and physical processes. We are already learning from biology in the fields of electronics and materials, but there is much more to be learned. The first nanotechnology applications will probably appear in the next few years in ultra-high-speed electronics. By allowing components to be smaller and circuits more densely packed, nanotechnology should be able to increase speeds in electronics even further. One promising approach is the use of carbon fullerene tubes as wires on a chip, linking together molecular-sized switches.

The dangers of nanotechnology are in some ways similar to those of genetic engineering. Nanomachines designed to rearrange or build organic molecules would not necessarily be benevolent to human beings and may even use us as raw materials.

In the long-term future, nanotechnology may be helpful for space exploration (see pages 88–9). By embedding our minds in a tiny capsule along with some universal assemblers – or nanotechnology machines designed to construct other nanotechnology machines – the size of a spacecraft could be reduced from hundreds of feet to a tiny fraction of an inch. Such devices could be accelerated close to the speed of light and sent off to explore by the million. On arrival at their selected destination, they could unpack nanomachines to assemble whatever is needed for habitation. Their final task would be to build an android into which they would upload their cargo, a human brain. Thus could the technologies of the very small and the very large be linked.

Current exploration of the universe (see **Space Exploration**, pages 88–9) is in its very early days. Although men landed on our moon 30 years ago, it will be many more years before humans will be ready to explore other planets in our solar system, let alone the planets of other stars. Only now are we starting to explore the earth's back yard, and since we cannot afford to send people, we can only do so by machine. With advanced artificial intelligence, space exploration by machine will be more effective. Machines will then be made that are much less vulnerable to hostile environments such as high g forces, extreme temperatures, unbreathable atmospheres or radiation. Real-time remote control is not feasible. The distances involved are so vast that artificially intelligent machines are needed that can act on their own initiative. The data gathered in future missions could be used to reconstruct a similar environment on earth, a secondhand, virtual reality experience.

The further we predict into the future, the less accurate our predictions become. The first generation of Star Trek used computing technology and voice synthesis that looks primitive by the standards of the late 1990s, but other Star Trek technologies, such as teleportation, belong to a distant future and may never be feasible. Most predictions more than a few years away are built only on quicksand, and their accuracy will depend heavily on luck.

Forecasting Methods

Most of the forecast data in this atlas have been derived by one or more of the methods described below. Information technology, though it cannot confer accuracy, is rapidly transforming the sophistication of forecasting techniques and applications.

Extrapolation is the most widely used method of forecasting. Built on the assumption that a pattern identified from the past will continue to operate, it provides a straightforward picture of what could happen in the future.

Such forecasts have a manifest clarity and certainty, but have meaning only if the future is indeed a continuation of the past. For this reason, extrapolations are often used to provide a base forecast. Forecasters then vary their assumptions, and develop alternatives.

Most extrapolative forecasting follows a time series. Quantitative data is collected that covers a period of time and is analyzed in search of recognizable patterns. The data may then be "smoothed" to eliminate the most significant variations and to identify underlying trends. Moving averages and exponential smoothing are two methods of reducing the extremes in data by creating a flatter line. In a third method, linear regression, a straight line is produced that statistically fits the data, with the minimum of divergence between the line and the actual readings. This works well where there is a clear linear trend and the data increases or decreases by a constant amount for each unit of time.

Trends are much more often measured in terms of percentage growth and decline. Exponential trends of this kind are unlikely to continue forever and tend to follow what is known as the growth- or S-curve. They show a pattern of growth that is initially fairly slow, and beyond a certain point explodes before decreasing and tailing off toward its limit. A series of S-curves is known as an envelope curve. This describes, for example, the way in which successive developments have extended the capability

of a particular technology. For example, the valve, transistor, and chip have successively extended the capability of electronics. Expressed as a forecast, the envelope curve assumes that further technological developments will continue the process.

There are other trends or patterns. Cycles, for example, are regular waves of fluctuation projected to repeat themselves into the future, as in business cycles. Precursor analysis suggests that trends in particular countries, states or firms, termed "Bellwethers," will provide a guide to future developments elsewhere.

Systems modelling is used to examine past events and the interaction of factors that brought them about. It can be used to test out alternative futures according to a variety of different assumptions, or to anticipate the consequences of different courses of action.

Speculation is intended to be thought provoking and to highlight potential opportunities and risks – such as developments within new technologies. It is often trend-based but it can also be innovative and challenge established wisdom. Speculation by its very nature embodies questions about what we or society really want.

Scenarios explore alternative futures and their likely consequences. These, too, are intended to provoke thought about the consequences of different courses of action rather than attempt to build accurate forecasts. There are many tried and tested tools available within scenario evaluation. Thought experiment uses human reasoning and experience, even intuition, to evaluate the likely path of change.

Some forecasting methods assume that judgment is the most significant factor. One of the most common, Delphi, assumes that collective expert judgment is the most valuable method of forecasting, using questionnaires interspersed by controlled feedback of opinions.

Contributors

Frank Barnaby
Former Director, Stockholm Peace Research Institute (SIPRI), Sweden. Nuclear physicist and former Research Director at the Atomic Weapons Research Establishment, Aldermaston, UK. Author of *Prospects for Peace*, New York and Oxford: Pergamon Press, 1980.

Sarah Bartlett
Assistant Managing Editor, *Business Week* magazine. Author of *The Money Machine: How KKR Manufactured Power and Profits*, New York: Warner Books, 1991.

Ben ten Brink
Coordinator for Biodiversity International, Rijksinstituut voor Volksgezondheid en Milieu (RIVM), Bilthoven, Netherlands. Author of the *Natural Capital Index* for UNEP's *Global Environment Outlook* and its Convention on Biological Diversity.

Dirk Bryant
Senior Associate, World Resources Institute, Washington DC. Co-author (with Daniel Nielsen and Laura Tangley) of *The Last Frontier Forests: Ecosystems and Economies on the Edge*, Washington DC: World Resources Institute, 1997.

Chris Buckley
Lecturer in Physics, King's College, University of London.

Simon Davies
Director General of Privacy International, Washington DC. Visiting Fellow, London School of Economics and Political Science (LSE); Visiting Fellow in Law, University of Essex. Author of *Big Brother: Britain's Web of Surveillance and the New Technological Order*, London: Pan Books, 1997.

Robert Engelman
Director of Population and Environment Program, Population Action International (PAI), Washington DC. Co-author (with Tom Gardner-Outlaw) of *Sustaining Water, Easing Scarcity: A Second Update*, Washington D.C.: Population Action International, 1997 and of *Plan and Conserve*, Washington DC: Population Action International, 1998.

Sandra Goldbeck-Wood
Papers editor, *British Medical Journal*, London.

Jeff Hecht
Science writer and correspondent for the *New Scientist* magazine. Co-author (with Christopher Scotese) of *The Ages of Earth: A 4-Billion-Year Atlas of Our Planet*, New York (forthcoming).

Kevin Kinsella
Chief of the Aging Studies Branch, International Programs Center, US Bureau of the Census. Author of *Older Workers, Retirement and Pensions*, Washington DC: US Department of Commerce, 1995 and *Population and Health Transitions*, Washington DC: US Department of Commerce, 1992.

Reinhard Loske
Senior Economist, Climate Policy Division, Wuppertal Institute for Climate, Environment and Energy, Wuppertal, Germany. Head of the institute's study group, Sustainable Germany.

Judith Mackay
Medical doctor and Director of the Asian Consultancy on Tobacco Control, Hong Kong. Author of *The State of Health Atlas*, New York and London: Simon & Schuster, 1993 and *The Sex Atlas* (forthcoming).

Robin Mannings
Chartered Engineer and Director of Intelligent
Transport Systems Research, BT Laboratories,
UK.

Angela Martins Oliveira
Statistician, Bureau of Statistics, International
Labour Organisation, Geneva.

Graham May
Principal Lecturer, Futures Research,
Leeds Metropolitan University, UK. Author of
*The Future Is Ours: Foreseeing, Managing and
Creating the Future,* London: Adamantine
Press, 1996.

Thomas Müller
Economist, Climate Policy Division,
Wuppertal Institute for Climate, Environment
and Energy, Wuppertal, Germany.

David Payne
Director of Optical Fiber Communications
Systems, BT Laboratories, UK. Director of the
Orwell Astronomical Society, Ipswich, UK.

Ian Pearson
Futurologist and Strategy Analyst,
BT Laboratories, Ipswich, UK. Co-author (with
Chris Winter) of *The Future of Communications*,
London: Thames and Hudson (forthcoming).

David Potter
Professor of Political Science, Open University,
Milton Keynes, UK. Co-editor of
Democratization, Cambridge: Polity Press,
1997.

Mark Rosegrant
Research Fellow, International Food Policy
Research Institute (IFPRI), Washington DC. Coordinator of research programs on water
resource policy and on agricultural investment
and productivity in Asia.

David Satterthwaite
Director of the Human Settlements Programme,
International Institute for Environment and
Development (IIED), London. Editor of the
journal *Environment and Urbanization.* Editor
and principal author of *An Urbanizing World:
Global Report on Human Settlements*, New York
and Oxford: Oxford University Press, 1996.

Roger Silverstone
Professor of Media and Communications,
London School of Economics and Political
Science (LSE). Editor of the journal *New Media
and Society.* Author of *Visions of Suburbia*,
London and New York: Routledge, 1997 and
Television and Everyday Life, London and New
York: Routledge, 1994.

Alan Smith
Reader, Department of Earth Sciences, and
Fellow, St John's College, University of
Cambridge, UK.

Lee J. Weddig
Former chief staff officer, National Fisheries
Institute, Arlington, VA. Founder of International
Coalition of Fisheries Association and of Global
Aquaculture Alliance. Former US Commissioner
to the International Commission for the
Conservation of Atlantic Tuna.

Chris Winter
Head of Future Systems Group,
BT Laboratories, UK and Director of Research
in optical systems, mobile telephony and
artificial intelligence. Visiting Professor of
Cybernetics, University of Reading, UK.

Sources

Part One: Earth

The Universe pages 10–11

Contributor: David Payne

Sources: • Clarke, Stuart, *Towards the Edge of the Universe*, Chichester: John Wiley & Sons, 1997 • Davis, Paul, ed., *The New Physics*, Cambridge: Cambridge University Press, 1989.

Spaceguard pages 12–13

Contributor: David Payne

Sources: • NASA Spaceguard Web page at http://ccf.arc.nasa.gov/sst/spaceguard.html • press reports.

Faultlines pages 14–15

Contributor: Alan Smith

Sources: • DeMets, C., R.G. Gordon, D.F. Argus and S. Stein, Current plate motions, *Geophysical Journal International*, 101 (1990): 425–78 • Simkin, T. and L. Siebert, *Volcanoes of the World: A Regional Directory, Gazetteer and Chronology During the Past 10,000 years*, 2nd edition, Phoenix, AZ: Arizona Geosciences Press Inc., 1994 • United Geological Survey CD-ROM of global hypocenter database for 1960–88.

Sea Change pages 16–17

Contributor: Jeff Hecht

Acknowledgments: • National Oceanic and Atmospheric Administration, Florida, USA.

Sources: • Climap Project, *Seasonal Reconstructions of the Earth's Surface at the Last Glacial Maximum*, Boulder, CO: Geological Society of America, 1981 • International Panel on Climate Change (IPCC), *Report 1995* at http://www.epa.gov/oppeoee1/globalwarming/actions/global/int ernational/ipcc.html • Scotese, Chris and Jeff Hecht, *Ages of Earth: A 4-Billion-Year Atlas of Our Planet*, forthcoming • United Nations Environment Programme (UNEP), *The Greenhouse Gases*, UNEP/Global Environment Monitoring System Environment Library no. 1, Nairobi, Bangladesh: 1987.

Global Warming pages 18–19

Contributor: Jeff Hecht

Sources: • Marland, Gregg and Tom Boden, Ranking of the world's countries by 1995 total CO_2 emissions from fossil-fuel burning, cement production, and gas flaring, Environmental Sciences Division, Oak Ridge National Laboratory, Oakridge, TN • Russell, Gary L., NASA/Goddard Institute for Space Studies at http://www.giss.nasa.gov/Data/

Ozone pages 20–1

Contributor: Jeff Hecht

Acknowledgments: • British Antarctic Survey, Cambridge, UK.

Sources: • Environment Canada at http://www.ns.doe.ca/udo/depl2.html • Jackman, Charles H. and others, Past, present, and future modeled ozone trends with comparisons to observed trends, *Journal of Geophysical Research*, no. 121 (December 20, 1996): 28, 753–8, 767 • Meteorological Organization, Scientific Assessment of Ozone Depletion, *Executive Summary* (NOAA, NASA, UNEP, and WMO), 1994 • NASA Goddard Space Flight Center at http://gcmd.gsfc.nasa.gov/faq/ozone.html • United Nations, Montreal Protocol, 1987 amended 1992 at http://www.ciesin.org/TG/PI/POLICY/montpro.html • US Environmental Protection Agency and Environment Canada data through http://gcmd.gsfc.nasa.gov/faq/ozone.html

Part Two: People

Population pages 24–5

Contributor: Kevin Kinsella

Sources: • US Bureau of the Census, International Data Base • press reports.

Lifetimes pages 26–7

Contributor: Kevin Kinsella

Sources: • US Bureau of the Census, International Data Base • press reports.

Superbugs pages 28–9

Contributor: Judith Mackay

Sources: • Garrett, Laurie, *The Coming Plague: Newly Emerging Diseases in a World out of Balance*, London: Virago, 1995 • Mackay, Judith, *The State of Health Atlas*, New York and London: Simon & Schuster, 1993 • Murray, Christopher J. L. and Alan D. Lopez, *The Global Burden of Disease: A Comprehensive Assessment of Mortality and Disability from Diseases, Injuries, and Risk Factors in 1990 and Projected to 2020*, Cambridge, MA: Harvard School of Public Health on behalf of the World Health Organization and the World Bank, 1996 • Pimentel, David and others, *Increasing Disease Incidence: Population Growth and Environmental Degradation*, Ithaca, NY: College of Agriculture and Life Sciences,Cornell University, 1997 • World Health Organization (WHO), *World Health Report 1996*, Geneva: WHO, 1997 • press reports.

Lifestyle Diseases pages 30–1

Contributor: Judith Mackay

Acknowledgments: • Saghir Bashir, International Agency for Research on Cancer, Unit of Descriptive Epidemiology, Lyon, France.

Sources: • Murray, Christopher J. L. and Alan D. Lopez, *The Global Burden of Disease: A Comprehensive Assessment of Mortality and Disability from Diseases, Injuries, and Risk Factors in 1990 and Projected to 2020*, Cambridge, MA: Harvard School of Public Health on behalf of the World Health Organization and the World Bank, 1996 • Peto, Richard and others, *Mortality from Smoking in Developed Countries, 1950–2000*, Oxford and New York: Oxford University Press, 1994 • World Health Organization (WHO), *World Health Report 1997*, Geneva: WHO, 1997.

High-Tech Health pages 32–3

Contributor: Judith Mackay

Sources: • *British Medical Journal*, various issues • *BT Technology Calendar 1997*, Ipswich: British Telecommunications, 1997 • internet • various medical and scientific journals • press reports.

Body Parts pages 34–5

Contributor: Judith Mackay

Sources: • BBC • *British Medical Journal* • *BT Technology Calendar 1997*, Ipswich: British Telecommunications, 1997 • various medical and scientific journals • press reports.

Artificial Intelligence pages 36–7

Contributor: Chris Winter

Sources: *BT Technology Calendar 1997*, Ipswich: British Telecommunications, 1997 • press reports.

New Conceptions pages 38–9

Contributor: Sandra Goldbeck-Wood

Sources: • American Society for Reproductive Medicine at http://www.asrm.com/current/press/embsplit.html • Center for Human Reproduction at http://www.centerforhumanreprod.com/art/ior/ior.htm • Human Fertilisation and Embryology Authority (HFEA), *Fifth Annual Report*, London: HFEA, July 1996 • World Health Organization (WHO), Division of Family Health, Programme on Maternal and Child Health and Family Planning, *Infertility*, Geneva: WHO, 1991.

Part Three: Resources

Forests pages 42–3

Contributors: Ben ten Brink; Dirk Bryant

Acknowledgments: Cees Klein Goldewijk and Eric Kreileman, RIVM; Daniel Nielsen, WRI.

Sources: • Bryant, Dirk, Daniel Nielsen and Laura Tangley, *The Last Frontier Forests: Ecosystems and Economies on the Edge*, Washington DC: World Resources Institute, 1997 • World Resources Institute, *World Resources 1996–97*, New York and Oxford: Oxford University Press, 1996 • United Nations Environment Programme (UNEP), *Global Environment Outlook*, Cambridge: Cambridge University Press, 1997.

Biodiversity pages 44–5

Contributor: Dirk Bryant

Acknowledgments: Daniel Nielsen, WRI.

Sources: • Bryant, Dirk and others, *Coastlines at Risk: An Index of Potential Development-Related Threats to Coastal Ecosystems*, Washington DC: World Resources Institute, Indicator Brief, 1995 • United Nations Environment Programme (UNEP), *Global Biodiversity Assessment*, Cambridge: Cambridge University Press, 1995 • World Resources Institute, *World Resources 1996–97*, New York and Oxford: Oxford University Press, 1996.

Water pages 46–7

Contributors: Mark W. Rosegrant; Robert Engelman

Acknowledgments: Claudia Ringler, IFPRI.

Sources: • Gardner-Outlaw, Tom and Robert Engelman, *Sustaining Water, Easing Scarcity: A Second Update*, Washington DC: Population Action International, 1997 • Rosegrant, Mark W., Claudia Ringler, and Roberta V. Gerpacio, Water and land resources, and global food supply, Paper prepared for the 23rd International Conference of Agricultural Economists, Sacramento, CA, August 10–16, 1997 • Rosegrant, Mark W., Dealing with water scarcity in the next century, *A 2020 Vision for Food, Agriculture and the Environment*, Brief 21 (June 1995).

Food pages 48–9

Contributor: Mark W. Rosegrant

Acknowledgments: Claudia Ringler, IFPRI.

Sources: • International Food Policy Research Institute (IFPRI), International Model for Policy Analysis of Agricultural Commodities and Trade (IMPACT) Projections • Rosegrant, Mark W. and Mercedita A. Sombilla, Critical issues suggested by trends in food, population, and the environment, *American Journal of Agricultural Economics,* vol. 79, no.5 (1997).

Note: The IMPACT model covers 37 countries and regions and 17 commodities, including cereals, roots and tubers, soybeans and meats, and is specified as a set of country-level supply and demand equations, with each country model linked to the rest of the world through trade.

Fishing pages 50–1

Contributor: Lee Weddig

Sources: • Food and Agriculture Organization (FAO), *FAO Yearbook: Fishery Statistics, Catchings and Landings*, vol. 80, Rome: FAO, 1995 • Food and Agriculture Organization (FAO), *Fisheries Series*, no. 48, Rome: FAO, 1997 • Food and Agriculture Organization (FAO), *FAO Statistics Series*, no. 134, Rome: FAO, 1997 • US Department of Commerce, National Oceanic and Atmospheric Administration, *Fisheries of the United States 1996*, Washington DC: US Department of Commerce, July 1997.

Energy pages 52–3

Contributors: Reinhard Loske and Thomas Müller

Sources: • International Energy Agency (IEA), *World Energy Outlook,* Paris: IEA, 1996.

The Internet pages 58–9

Contributor: Ian Pearson

Sources: • TeleGeography Inc. • Network Wizards at http://www.nw.com/zone/WWW/top.html

Media pages 60–1

Contributor: Roger Silverstone

Sources: • *ATM Magazine,* no. 4 (April 1,1997): 12, 14, 22 • *Screen Digest* (March 1997): 57–64 • Shepherd, Lloyd, European cable and satellite flying high, *Broadcasting & Cable International*, October and December 1995 • UNESCO, *Statistical Yearbook,* New York: UN, 1996 • press reports.

Surveillance pages 62–3

Contributor: Simon Davies

Sources: • Agre, Philip and Marc Rotenberg, eds., *Technology and Privacy: The New Landscape*, Cambridge, MA: MIT Press, 1997 • Davies, Simon, *Big Brother: Britain's Web of Surveillance and the New Technological Order*, London: Pan Books,1997 • *The International Privacy Bulletin*, Washington DC: Privacy International, 1994–98 • Quittner, Joshua, Invasion of privacy, *Time* (August, 25 1997): 40–7 • *World Human Rights Reports*, 1995–97, Washington DC: US State Department • *The World in 1997*, London: The Economist, 1996.

Traffic pages 64–5

Contributor: Robin Mannings

Sources: • CIA, *World Fact Book*, Washington DC: CIA, 1997 • Schafer, Andreas and David Victor, The Past and future of global mobility, *Scientific American* (October 1997): 36–9.

Part Four: Communications

The Wired World pages 56–7

Contributor: Ian Pearson

Acknowledgments: • Jon Wakeling, BT Laboratories, Ipswich, UK.

Sources: • International Telecommunications Union (UIT), *Nouvelles de l'Uit*, no. 1 (1996) • Maroney, Tyler, Info pipelines, *Time* (3 February 1997): 38-9 • TeleGeography Inc. • The World Bank, *World Bank Atlas, 1997*, Washington DC: International Bank for Reconstruction and Development/The World Bank, 1997 • press reports • websites: http://leonardo.jpl.nasa.gov/msl/QuickLooks/odysseyQL.html • http://www.ee.surrey.ac.uk/Personal/L.Wood/constellations/ • http://www.iridium.com/systm/systm.html

Part Five: Globalization

Tourism pages 68–9

Contributor: Ian Pearson

Acknowledgments: • Robin Mannings, Chris Winter, BT Laboratories, Ipswich, UK.

Sources: • Branegan, Jay, Tourism is working: special report, *Time* (June 16, 1997) • World Tourism Organization (WTO), *Tourism 2020 Vision: Influences, Directional Flows and Key Trends*, executive summary, Madrid: WTO, 1997.

Work pages 70–1

Contributor: Angela Martins Oliveira

Sources: • International Labour Organisation (ILO), Bureau of Statistics, *Economically Active Population, 1950–2010,* 5 vols. working papers, Geneva: ILO, 1997 • press reports.

Business pages 72–3

Contributor: Sarah Bartlett

Sources: • Bank for International Settlements (BIS), *Central Bank Survey of Foreign Exchange and Derivatives Market Activity,* Basel, Switzerland: BIS, 1995 • Hatem, Fabrice, *International Investment: Towards the Year 2001,* Paris: UN in cooperation with DATAR, UNCTAD and Arthur Andersen, Inc., 1997 • IMD, *World Competitiveness Yearbook,* Lausanne, Switzerland: IMD, 1997 • United Nations Conference on Trade and Development (UNCTAD), *World Investment Report 1997: Transnational Corporations, Market Structure and Competition Policy,* Geneva and New York: UNCTAD,1997.

Cities pages 74–5

Contributor: David Satterthwaite

Sources: • Satterthwaite, David, *The Scale and Nature of Urban Change in the South,* London: International Institute for Environment and Development (IIED), 1996 • United Nations Population Division, *World Urbanization Prospects: The 1994 Revision,* New York: UN, 1995 • United Nations Development Programme (UNDP), *The Human Development Report,* New York and Oxford: Oxford University Press, 1993.

Economies pages 76–7

Acknowledgments: • Stephen Burman, University of Sussex, Brighton, UK.

Sources: • Economist Intelligence Unit (EIU), *Global Outlook 1997,* London: EIU, 1997 • Garten, Jeffrey E., *The Big Ten: The Big Emerging Markets and How They Will Change Our Lives,* New York: HarperCollins, Basic Books, 1997 • International Monetary Fund (IMF), *World Economic Outlook,* Washington DC: IMF, May 1997.

Democracy pages 78–9

Contributor: David Potter

Sources: • Potter, David and others, *Democratization,* Cambridge: Polity Press, 1997 • Dahl, R., *Democracy and Its Critics,* New Haven, CT: Yale University Press, 1989.

Military Might pages 80–1

Contributor: Frank Barnaby

Sources: • International Institute for Strategic Studies (IISS), *The Military Balance 1996–97,* London: IISS, 1997 • Stockholm International Peace Research Institute (SIPRI), *Yearbook,* New York and Oxford: Oxford University Press, various dates • press reports.

United Nations pages 82–3

Contributor: Frank Barnaby

Sources: • International Institute for Strategic Studies (IISS), *The Military Balance 1996–97,* London: IISS, 1997 • Stockholm International Peace Research Institute (SIPRI), *Yearbook,* New York and Oxford: Oxford University Press, various dates.

Part Six: Into the Unknown

Nanotechnology pages 86–7

Contributor: Ian Pearson

Sources: • Stix, Gary, Trends in nanotechnology: waiting for breakthroughs, *Scientific American,* April 1996: 78-83 • Kurian, George Thomas and Graham T. Molitor, eds., *Encyclopedia of the Future,* New York: Macmillan, 1996 • press reports.

Space Exploration pages 88–9

Contributor: Chris Buckley

Sources: • British Astronomical Association at http://www.ast.cam.ac.uk/~baa • NASA at http://nssdc.gsfc.nasa.gov/planetary/ • various space science journals • press reports.

Forecasting Methods page 119

Contributor: Graham May

Source: • May, Graham, *The Future Is Ours: Foreseeing, Managing and Creating the Future,* Westport, CT: Praeger; London: Adamantine Press, 1996.

Organizations

The following organizations have provided forecast data for this atlas:

• Economist Intelligence Unit (EIU), London
• International Energy Agency (IEA), Paris
• International Food Policy Research Institute (IFPRI), Washington DC
• International Labour Organisation (ILO), Geneva
• International Monetary Fund (IMF), Washington DC
• Rijksinstituut voor Volksgezondheid en Milieu (RIVM): "National Institute for Public Health and Environmental Protection," Bilthoven, Netherlands
• Population Action International (PAI), Washington DC
• Privacy International, Washington DC
• World Health Organization (WHO), Geneva
• World Resources Institute (WRI), Washington DC
• World Tourist Organization (WTO), Madrid
• US Bureau of the Census (Population Division: International Programs Center), Washington DC.

Index